Praise for *Build Your Money Muscles* . . .

"Possibly the best book on money ever written."

—Hugh Prather
Author of *Morning Notes, Shining Through,*
and *The Little Book of Letting Go*

"An extremely valuable book for those who have issues with money. It is full of practical advice, and I heartily recommend it for anyone who wants to know more about themselves and their relationship with money."

—Susan Jeffers, Ph.D.
Author of *Feel the Fear* and *Do It Anyway* and *Life is Huge!*

"A great book for those who are serious about financial success. Joan illuminates the behaviors people use to sabotage their financial health, while providing solid strategies for positive change."

—John F. Brunett, Jr.
Certified Financial Planner

"Health and wealth are intimately connected. *Build Your Money Muscles* provides a step-by-step process to shore up your ability to attract and manage money healthfully."

—Christiane Northrup, M.D.
Author of *Mother-Daughter Wisdom, The Wisdom of Menopause,*
and *Women's Bodies, Women's Wisdom*

"Joan is insightful, practical, and down to earth. . . . If you are truly ready to redefine your relationship with money in new and healthy ways, this book is a wonderful guide."

—Justine Willis
Cofounder and managing producer,
New Dimensions World Broadcasting Network,
and coauthor, with Michael Toms, of *True Work*

"For the millions of baby boomers clueless about how to plan for a future that won't include traditional retirement, Joan Sotkin's *Build Your Money Muscles* is a gift [leading] the way to financial independence that makes choice possible."

—Marika and Howard Stone
Coauthors of *Too Young to Retire*

"There are hundreds of books out there about making money. What differentiates this one is that it takes the reader through exercises allowing actual participation in the learning process. I heartily recommend *Build Your Money Muscles* for anyone with a desire to grow financially."

—Patricia B. Murray
Senior Vice President, First State Bank New Mexico

"*Build Your Money Muscles* is critical for anyone who faces a wall of resistance around mature money handling. Thanks to this fine work, financial issues no longer have to keep you from your dreams."

—Suzanne Falter-Barns
Author of *How Much Joy Can You Stand?* and *Living Your Joy*

"As a broker, I see people every day who could earn far more from their businesses if they followed the advice in *Build Your Money Muscles*. Anyone who is considering building a business should read this book."

—Sam Goldenberg
Business broker

"A practical, insightful handbook for creating a new financial awareness and more effective habits. Joan's wisdom on this topic is transformative."

—Gail McMeekin, LICSW
Author of *The 12 Secrets of Highly Creative Women*
and *Creative Success Newsletter*

BUILD YOUR MONEY MUSCLES

Nine Simple Exercises
for Improving Your Relationship with Money

JOAN SOTKIN

Prosperity
Place

Santa Fe, New Mexico

Published by: Prosperity Place, Inc.
                PO Box 22993
                Santa Fe, NM 87502

Editor: Ellen Kleiner
Book design and typography: Janice St. Marie
Illustrations: Jaye Oliver
Cover design: Janice St. Marie

Copyright © 2006 by Joan Sotkin

Printed in the United States of America on acid-free recycled paper

Publisher's Cataloging-in-Publication Data

Sotkin, Joan.
          Build your money muscles : nine simple exercises for improving
          your relationship with money / Joan Sotkin. -- 1st ed. -- Santa Fe, N.M. :
          Prosperity Place, 2006.
          p. ; cm.
          Includes bibliographical references.
          ISBN: 0-9741719-8-0
          ISBN: 978-0-9741719-8-2
          ISBN: 0-9741719-6-4 (softcover)
          ISBN: 978-0-9741719-6-8 (softcover)

          1. Finance, Personal. 2. Budgets, Personal. I. Title.

HG179 .S68 2005   2004116458
332.024--dc22   0504
10 9 8 7 6 5 4 3 2 1

To the Santa Fe Prosperity Circle,
for their inspiring support and encouragement
and their willingness to move into new financial identities

Acknowledgments

First and foremost, I want to thank Ellen Kleiner for her patient prodding, empathetic counsel, and superb editing, all of which were essential to the publication of this book. I also greatly appreciate the help I received from Ellen's assistant, Hillary Welles.

None of this information could have been developed without the encouragement of the many visitors to ProsperityPlace.com, as well as my coaching clients who were willing to hear what I had to say and try the various techniques I suggested. I was constantly inspired by their ongoing feedback and willingness to trust my guidance.

The TEC (The Executive Committee) group—an international community of CEOs—I joined in October 2004, and especially its able leader Les Samuels, further stimulated my expansion, provided me with invaluable practical knowledge, and gave me the support and encouragement I needed to move forward with this project. It's an honor to have Pam Duncan, Stefan Lark, Charlie Goodman, Stan Singley, Paul Benson, Leon Romero, Jennifer Adelman, and Tom Jensen as part of my executive committee.

Contents

Actions

Preface

*B*uild *Your Money Muscles* evolved from techniques I devised
to bring myself from financial dysfunction, characterized
by under-earning and compulsive debting, to financial comfort.
During this transformation, I discovered that the only way to
alter my financial condition was by going through corresponding
internal changes. Consequently, I gradually altered my approach
to life and reframed my concept of who I was and my place in the
world. Unearthing a significant connection between emotions
and money, I then developed methods for using it to improve my
financial position.

I began my quest because I wanted to understand why I had
so much trouble functioning financially, while my two younger
brothers could both manage money effectively. In 1983, one of
my brothers, tired of having to rescue me financially, suggested
I enroll in a Twelve-Step program. I soon discovered Debtors
Anonymous (DA), where I was introduced to the concept that
I was using debting as an emotional fix and that to understand
the cause of my under-earning and debting I had to examine the
emotions behind my behaviors. The DA program worked well for
me, and by 1984 I had started a wholesale, retail, and mail-order
business that ended up grossing over $325,000 in its fourth year.

Following my father's death in 1987, however, I rapidly
reverted to old behaviors, such as buying excessive inventory on
credit, and ultimately amassed a $40,000 debt. Less than a year
later, I closed the business and filed for bankruptcy. Realizing I had
to look further into my emotions and their effect on my financial
behavior, I began attending Codependents Anonymous (CoDA),
where I came to better understand the underlying causes for my

dysfunction. I recognized that I had been unable to effectively grieve the death of my father and had therefore created a situation that let me express grief by losing a business I loved. Also, I could see that because I had previously experienced a sudden influx of a large amount of money without the benefit of a financial education, I had been overwhelmed, which led to overspending and poor business decisions.

As a result of losing my business, I gained a deep awareness of my financial attitudes and behaviors and set about deliberately building money muscles by developing both the inner and outer resources I needed to become financially healthy and successful. I now understand that prosperity is not only about money but also about feeling comfortable, satisfied, and secure, and that sustaining prosperity requires both an ongoing financial education and a willingness to deal with the responsibilities and many changes that come with material wealth.

To share what I learned during my transformation, in 1995 I developed a Web site, ProsperityPlace.com, where to this day I teach a holistic approach to improved relationships with money. The thousands of people who visit this site each month are interested in increasing their income and fostering abundance in every aspect of their lives, even though most have never had a surplus of funds and many are in debt. On the site they learn that even with extensive financial knowledge, neglecting to prepare emotionally for the life changes that come with increased income makes it difficult to either build or sustain wealth.

The theory behind *Build Your Money Muscles* is that an individual's finances are an extension of their concept about who they are and their place in the world. Generating and managing increasingly large sums of money requires understanding your finances in this context, as well as gradually developing money management skills. The exercises presented in this book are divided into two sections. Part I, "Preparation for Financial Change," is designed to help you understand the dynamics behind your current financial situation, raise your level of financial awareness, and set realistic goals for your future. Part II, "Toward a New Financial Identity," provides techniques for altering your relationships with yourself and others in order to establish healthy financial habits. Each exercise ends with a series of actions that can be practiced independently for increased financial stability.

The book concludes with a listing of resources, including many helpful Web sites. In addition, ProsperityPlace.com offers related articles, audio programs, e-books, and prosperity tips.

May your new fitness routine awaken long-dormant muscle groups and offer ongoing fortification as you dramatically alter your financial position and develop a more comfortable, free-flowing, and functional relationship with money.

PART I

Preparation
for
Financial
Change

INTRODUCTION

Why can one person easily generate and manage large sums of money while another struggles to barely cover basic expenses? This question propelled me on a search for the dynamics governing money and our relationship with it. After years of studying, observing, and working with hundreds of people, I began to formulate answers. I saw that a person's financial condition depends not on external factors, such as how much money they earn and invest, but on their internal environment, which includes who they perceive themselves to be, how they think, and what they need to express emotionally. Our relationship with money, I concluded, reflects more about our thoughts, beliefs, and feelings than it does about the world of finance.

With individual clients and in groups I facilitated, I was able to test this theory and develop simple techniques for cultivating a happier relationship with money and choosing a satisfying financial pathway. Instead of initially focusing on money management skills, we examined and altered thought patterns, habitual beliefs, and emotional responses, causing the participants to shift their concept of themselves and their place in the world. They gradually began to adopt new financial habits and, almost without effort, experience a healthier money flow because their finances automatically reflected their new-found expressions of self-worth.

The theory behind the exercises in Part I presumes that financial situations do not just happen to us but are instead created by our deeply embedded and often unexpressed thoughts, beliefs, and emotions (TBEs). Accepting this theory allows us to see that conditions such as being underpaid, getting laid off, facing unexpected expenses, having no savings, or losing money, all of which seem caused by external circumstances, are instead extensions of our internal world and our relationships with ourselves and others. The cornerstones of this theory are that behind every financial situation there lies a set of thoughts, beliefs, and emotions (see figure I–1), and that people subconsciously draw in whatever and whomever they need to give external expression to this internal condition.

Figure I–1 What thoughts, beliefs, and emotions contribute to your financial situation?

Thirty-five-year-old Sam, due to his past experiences, believes that people cannot be trusted. As a result, when interacting with others Sam often fears being cheated, lied to, or otherwise taken advantage of, and he expects he will be disappointed, betrayed, and victimized, as he was previously. According to the theoretical underpinnings of this preparation program, Sam's combination of TBEs is sending out a nonverbal message likely to attract people into his life who will validate his unarticulated fears and expectations. He in turn will most likely blame his resulting distress on others, not realizing it was his thoughts, beliefs, and emotions that set the groundwork for his sense of victimization. Once Sam accepts his situation as an expression of his hidden TBEs, he will be able to reexamine his interactions with others from this new point of view, make a conscious effort to alter his TBEs, and foster more comfortable outcomes.

When viewed through the lens of unaddressed TBEs, forty-two-year-old Evan's situation is similarly illuminating. When Evan was three years old, his brother Luke was born, displacing him as the center of his mother's attention. Evan then discovered he could get his mother to notice him by being disruptive—behavior that led to criticism and punishment. In response to his mother's reactions, he came to believe there was something inherently wrong with him. He often repeated to himself her words of admonishment: "You never do anything right," "You shouldn't act that way," and "What's the matter with you?" These thoughts, coupled with the underlying belief that he was in some way deficient, led to feelings of shame, inadequacy, and unworthiness.

Although disruptive at home, Evan was a good student, and he eventually earned a degree in chemistry, after which he accepted a job in a research laboratory. While he enjoyed working at the lab, he considered himself underpaid and often worried about paying off his student loan and the credit card bills he was accruing. Then three years after taking the job, Evan was laid off and replaced by another chemist. Once again he felt ashamed, inadequate, unworthy, and now trapped financially as well.

It might appear that Evan's employment history and financial bind were caused by bad luck or poor planning. Viewed from the perspective of this theory, however, it was Evan's TBEs that were the creative force behind his employment dramas and financial hardships. His concept of himself as deficient and unworthy, coupled with his self-critical judgments and pent-up feelings of shame, inadequacy, and unworthiness led him to unconsciously attract the circumstances needed to help him express his under-lying anger and resentment about being displaced early in his life. From this vantage point, his layoff, years of being underpaid, and the burden of debt he carried can all be seen as expressions of feelings long repressed. As Evan learns to release his inhibited emotions and change the tenor of his thoughts, he will be prepared to develop a more supportive relationship with himself and no longer need to be plagued with discomforting financial dramas. In response, he will most likely find a better-paying job and manage his money more skillfully.

Along with accepting that his TBEs create his financial situa-tion, Evan can also benefit by understanding the nature of money. Although it strongly influences human lives—affecting decisions about housing, food, leisure time, employment, health care, and much more—by itself money has no power. Only when used as a medium of exchange does money acquire potency, and its use creates a relationship between those involved in each transaction (see figure I-2). In other words, money represents the energy of relationship, and the way individuals handle money reflects how they deal with their relationships with themselves and others.

Figure I–2 Money represents energy passing between two people and generates a relationship between them.

Apparent financial problems, then, are never about money and always about relationships, and financial relationships invariably have an emotional base. As such, feelings of financial insecurity, while appearing to be about money, may in fact represent a sense of disconnectedness from oneself and others, fear of being left alone, or some other relationship concern. And the willingness to address these issues can prevent lack of funds from becoming a chronic or recurring condition.

Twenty-eight-year-old Karen, for example, was perennially in debt and struggling to earn enough through her business to cover her expenses. Every few months, afraid of having her service discontinued, Karen would nervously call either the phone or utility company to ask for more time to pay her bill. Her relationship with these firms mirrored her relationship with her parents, whom she often asked to rescue her from financial disaster. On those occasions of protracted pleading and sobbing, her parents would grudgingly give her money, whereupon she would temporarily feel less alone and unworthy. Now when Karen needed to feel connected and appreciated, conversations with the phone or utility company personnel substituted for interactions with her parents. From the outside it appeared she had a problem generating enough money, but underneath lay an unfulfilled relationship with her parents.

Once Karen understood that to feel connected and worthy she needed to develop healthy relationships, she made a concerted effort to widen her circle of social contacts by joining a local singles hiking group and becoming active in a women's business networking organization. A month later, she began gradually focusing on her relationship with money by keeping better financial records, examining and releasing the emotions behind her financial patterns, and learning about cash-flow management for her business. Within a year, Karen's revenues had improved dramatically, and in retrospect she realized the most significant shifts she underwent were a growing sense of trust, support, and love for herself, along with new feelings of belonging in her relationships with others—all of which were reflected in her new relationship with money.

Just as Karen used the phone and utility companies to externalize her relationship issues with her family, people adopt a variety of vehicles for emotional expression. Applying for a bank loan, for instance, causes many borrowers to feel like a child asking a parent for more allowance. Similarly, employee-employer and customer-proprietor interactions, although financial in nature, often reenact family dynamics. From this point of view, it makes sense that individuals who felt undervalued as children might perceive themselves as being underpaid or overcharged as adults.

Interestingly debt, which appears as a financial state, actually allows both the debtor and lender to express hidden emotions. Debtors often harbor feelings of being controlled, trapped, inadequate, powerless, or ashamed, while lenders, after advancing money to a debtor, can feel more potent and commanding than they do in other situations. Both debtors and lenders, feeling less alienated because of their financial bond, generally benefit from these relationships until they are able to find a more intimate means of emotional expression.

Indeed, money frequently represents an aspect of love. Parents affectionately pass money on to their children; donors support their favorite charities; and employers give bonuses as a gesture of caring and appreciation. By contrast, money can also be a medium through which people express their need for love. Individuals who were abused or neglected as children often act out their absence of love and nurturing through a history of insufficient funds, underearning, or requests to be rescued by family, friends, or credit card companies. Similarly, people who routinely lend money may be expressing the need to be loved, perceiving that their generosity will inspire fondness among borrowers.

Examining the sentiments expressed through your finances can lead to a more satisfying relationship with money. Improving your relationship with money in an enduring way, however, requires altering habitual attitudes and behaviors, which takes time and experimentation. By envisioning money as a being with whom you will have lifelong interactions, you will understand the value of learning to love, respect, care for, and appreciate money and its place in your life. When you do this, money, like people you value, will be drawn to you more easily, infusing your life with enhanced joy and fulfillment.

The following preparation program for financial change is rooted in the theory that thoughts, beliefs, and emotions create reality and that new thoughts, beliefs, and emotions create a new reality. Along with offering suggestions for developing financial skills, the exercises address developing TBEs congruent with financial comfort, and finding alternative avenues of expression for the TBEs causing financial dysfunction. Like the exercises in any weight-lifting program, these are designed to be done gradually and repeatedly over an extended period of time. Imagine a 125-pound sedentary woman who has never lifted weights suddenly exercising with a 20-pound dumbbell in each hand. She could easily strain a muscle or give up out of frustration and disappointment. Likewise, most people drawn to prosperity literature hope to generate large sums of money quickly, without realizing that practice "lifting" larger and larger sums of money is required to mitigate the demands of prosperity. Stories abound about lottery winners who after a few years are back where they started or entrepreneurs who rapidly build successful businesses only to watch them crash. Suddenly inheriting, earning, or winning large sums of money often leaves the recipient feeling overwhelmed and rendered financially dysfunctional by the abrupt infusion of funds.

With money, as with dumbbells, it makes sense to gradually develop the "muscles" needed to safely and comfortably reach increasingly higher levels of proficiency. The exercises in Part I help you do that by gradually boosting your financial awareness and aptitude while enhancing your understanding of the internal blocks holding you back from sustained wealth. In removing these blocks, you naturally become better equipped to support yourself and manage money well—stepping stones to not only a rosier financial future but a more satisfying life.

Conditioning Yourself
for Change

If we don't change, we don't grow.
If we don't grow, we are not really living.
—GAIL SHEEHY

Effective exercise programs include conditioning routines to assist in adapting to new muscle movements and mental challenges. Likewise, a reliable preparation program for financial fitness incorporates activities that help minimize the discomforts involved in moving to a new financial position. Such discomforts arise largely from encounters with resistance. And because it stimulates ongoing internal and external changes, reaching for an improved financial position provides ample opportunity for resistance.

Most prosperity seekers, while wanting their lives to improve significantly, resist change because they derive comfort from the relatively predictable financial patterns they have known. But, unwilling to endure temporary discomfort, they remain blocked from achieving financial satisfaction and freedom. Fortunately, by understanding the factors prompting your resistance and by consciously preparing for change, you can gradually alter the habitual thoughts, beliefs, emotions, and behaviors that are keeping you stuck in your current financial position.

Threats Posed by the Identity Factor

A primary reason for resistance rests with what I have named the Identity Factor, an internal mechanism that protects a person's concept of who they are and their place in the world. Moving to a new financial position, which can easily threaten one's sense of self, often activates the Identity Factor. When this happens, people typically either procrastinate or revert to old behaviors, protecting their familiar lifestyle at all costs for fear that their desired changes, when they finally do occur, will leave them feeling alienated, unsafe, and confused.

Sharon, who was committed to getting out of debt and establishing healthy financial habits, was unaware of the potential discomforts triggered by change. With the help of a credit counselor, Sharon devised a plan to gradually eliminate her credit card debt, stop using credit cards, and keep better financial records. For three months, she faithfully followed the program and delighted in the progress she saw; but in the fourth month, she started slipping behind in her payments and twice borrowed money from a friend. Ashamed, she stopped keeping track of her spending and within six months was back where she had started, increasing her debt, avoiding financial tasks, and only vaguely aware of her expenditures.

When she first called me, Sharon was disappointed in herself for sabotaging her progress. Once she understood she had been protecting her old identity, however, she realized her actions were not self-sabotaging but self-protective. She saw that because she did not recognize herself as a person who behaved responsibly with money, she had protected her identity by resorting to familiar behaviors with more predictable outcomes. Over time, she learned how to work through the discomfort imposed by changed behaviors and began to develop new TBEs, all of which helped her recommit to her financial plan.

Along with threatening a person's self-concept, significant change can also affect peer and family-of-origin relationships. Since people know you as the person you once were, any change in your attitudes or behaviors requires them to respond to you differently, and consequently undergo a change of their own. Friends or family members who are not amenable to changing might try to stymie your progress—a situation likely to compound your discomfort with fears of ultimately being left alone. Fortunately, while conditioning yourself for change you will see that being alone is not inevitable. You can always redefine earlier relationships with friends and family, and also develop new relationships with people reflecting your changed state of being, who will invariably come into your life.

Accepting the Moving Stupids

Initiating a move to a new financial position by altering habitual TBEs and behaviors can be disorienting at first because the itinerary and outcome are both uncertain. If you have ever moved from one dwelling to another, you have probably experienced what I call the "moving stupids." Symptoms include feeling overwhelmed, confused, alone, lost, and likely to misplace things or make unwise decisions. Just as you adapt to your surroundings after moving to a new house, however, the discomforts caused by altered TBEs and financial behaviors will gradually subside. Embracing the moving stupids as a sign of progress toward a new financial position can reduce their duration and help propel you forward.

At age fifty-four, Larry was ready to redefine his relationship with money. Although he yearned for financial stability, he felt trapped by his debt and ashamed of his vagueness about finances. When he first started working with me, Larry agreed to stop using his credit cards, follow a spending plan we devised, and keep track of everything he spent. After only two weeks, he felt anxious and disoriented and confessed to two bouts of binge eating. "I have a raging case of the moving stupids," he lamented. "I feel good about what I'm doing, but I'm having trouble deciding what to spend money on. I'm so afraid I'll make a mistake and overspend. And when I'm writing down my spending for the day, it feels as if someone else is in my body. I'm not used to behaving this way."

At last reassured that the discomforts would pass, Larry agreed to continue the new behaviors. At the end of another two weeks, he told me that the disorientation and indecision were gradually diminishing and his new behaviors felt more natural. Still, every time Larry introduced a new behavior, such as saving money from each paycheck, he had twinges of disorientation. But because he understood that the moving stupids indicated progress and would soon pass, he was willing to go through the experience.

Actions

The following actions are designed to assist in overcoming resistance and can help condition you for change by expanding your self-awareness. Be patient as you make changes. Also adapt to small shifts before attempting larger ones. Any time you feel a sense of resistance, avoid criticizing yourself; instead, relax and prepare to renew your efforts.

1. Create a prosperity journal

A prosperity journal is an ideal place for defining your current situation and tracking your progress as you build your money muscles. Use it also to record your fears or resistance, affirm your successes, make note of questions that arise, or express your reactions to change. Dating each entry facilitates a later analysis of your observations.

2. Find a prosperity buddy

Enlisting the help of a friend to work with can increase your motivation to minimize discomforts and make your progress to a new financial position more enjoyable. Choose someone with whom you feel comfortable sharing personal information. Agree to exchange experiences once or twice a week for a specified amount of time, such as thirty minutes per session, divided equally between you. The sessions will ideally take place either in person or on the phone to allow for immediate feedback. During each one, take turns noting the progress made since the last session, describing the discomforts experienced such as alienation or disorientation, asking for feedback if desired, and declaring what you will do before the next session. Avoid judging your buddy's behavior or giving unsolicited advice, which may only lead to conflict. Instead, give encouragement by praising your buddy's progress.

For couples, it is a good idea to select prosperity buddies outside of the relationship, especially if your financial discussions tend to be emotional. You can work on your money issues together, but having an outsider as a confidant is likely to encourage each of you to be more honest about your personal struggles.

People who use a buddy system tend to progress more quickly than those who do not. Sharing information about financial behavior, an uncommon practice, opens up new avenues of authentic expression for participants and often releases considerable shame associated with financial habits.

3. Define your financial identity

Your financial identity, which can easily feel threatened by change, is made up of your thoughts, beliefs, emotions, behaviors, and your relationship with money. Gaining clarity about your financial identity can assist you in recognizing signs of resistance to financial change and in dealing with the disorientation that is likely to occur as your financial position advances.

To begin, following the format shown in figure 1-1, profile each component of your financial identity, as you understand it, in your prosperity journal, leaving space for future entries. Valuable information can be gleaned by listening for statements you repeatedly make about your finances, especially those starting with "I," such as "I'm never going to make enough money" or "I feel stuck." In listing your behaviors, notice whether you avoid taking financial risks or tend instead to be more confident. Are you generous or prone to stinginess? Do you have a positive or negative outlook toward your financial future?

4. Make one small external change

Intentionally altering a relatively insignificant behavior and then observing your inner responses to it can help you adapt to new financial behaviors. Here are some possibilities:

- Put your toothbrush in a different place.
- Take an unfamiliar street to a destination you frequently travel to.
- Get up a few minutes earlier than usual, or stay up a bit later.
- Watch a different news channel.
- Read a magazine you have never seen before.
- Replace one serving of cake or ice cream with a healthier snack.
- Smile at someone you do not know.
- Go to a meeting you've been thinking about attending.

My Financial Identity	
Thoughts	I wish I had more money. If only I could borrow money from my parents. My finances are a mess. Why can't I get what I want? I'm broke. I hate having to think about money so much. I don't know how to make ends meet.
Beliefs	I don't deserve to have a lot of money. Everybody earns a decent income but me. If I make extra money, I won't know what to do with it. I'm not very good with money.
Emotions	When it comes to money, I feel frustrated, unworthy, inadequate, unhappy, and fearful.
Behaviors	I'm not good about keeping financial records. I don't know where all my money goes. I keep using my credit cards even though I know I shouldn't. I let my bills pile up without looking at them. I sometimes forget to pay my bills.
Relationship with Money	Conflicted, unsure, lacking

Figure 1–1

- Reverse the toilet paper roll in your bathroom.
- Eat a food you have never tried before.
- Use a different brand of automobile fuel.
- Shop at a grocery store you have never before frequented.
- Listen to some new music.
- Talk to someone you have been avoiding.

Repeat the new action daily until you are comfortable with it. All the while, notice any feelings of disorientation and how long it takes you to ultimately adapt to the change. For some people the discomfort lasts only a few days, whereas for others it can go on for weeks. After establishing your particular pace, you will be able to predict with some certainty how long the identity threats and moving stupids will persist as you initiate more new behaviors.

5. Change one financial behavior

To condition yourself for financial growth, take one small step toward managing your money differently. Possibilities include the following:

- Write down how much money you earn and spend in one day.
- Pay a week's worth of bills on time.
- Stop using your favorite credit card.
- Save money you would normally spend, even if it is only a dollar a week.
- Give some money away.
- Go for one day without spending money.

As you make this change, notice your feelings and record them in your prosperity journal. If you are aware of discomfort but unable to associate it with particular feelings, for now just document the discomfort.

6. Examine any resistance to financial change

If you resisted performing the previous action, ask yourself these questions:

- How will making a financial change affect my feelings about myself?
- What am I afraid might happen if I achieve financial success?
- Will feeling financially secure threaten my concept of myself? Will it alter my relationships with my peers or family of origin?
- Would my prosperity signify betrayal to a peer, or perhaps disloyalty to a family member?

7. Work with a "power word"

The subconscious mind accepts what it is told and uses these beliefs to bring forth outcomes. If you tell your subconscious mind that life provides opportunities, you will have opportunities; tell it that you never get what you want and disappointment will prevail. Contradictory beliefs, however, can cause interference, as can resistance to change. For example, if I tell my subconscious mind that I am experiencing an easy cash flow yet I harbor the conflicting belief that it is difficult for me to make money, no matter how often I reinforce my perception of an easy cash flow, it will be obstructed. Likewise, fear or any other uncomfortable emotion I might have about the effects of an easy cash flow could also hinder a positive outcome. Fortunately, because the subconscious mind believes and acts on what it is told, it can be taught to release old beliefs and unhealthy emotions and move through resistance.

To harness the participation of your subconscious mind as you condition your money muscles, practice the following technique—a method based on the Be Set Free Fast (BSFF) approach developed by psychologist Larry Nims. First, choose what I call a "power word," which can be any word or short phrase that, unlike the word *money*, perhaps, does not have a strong emotional charge for you. My power word is *terrific*. Examples of terms my coaching clients have used include *Shazam, Freedom, Peace, Do it*, and *Go, girl*.

Next, read the following statement aloud to alert your subconscious mind to the outcomes you would like it to present.

> *Subconscious mind, every time I notice a problem, discomfort, belief, or behavior I intend to release, you will employ the following power word to eliminate all the roots of the problem, emotional discomfort, belief, or behavior.*

*You will also apply this power word to install any state-
ment of intention, affirmation, or new belief that I make.
The power word I am going to use is _____.*

If you later decide to change your power word, repeat the statement and conclude by saying, "Subconscious mind, I am now
going to use the power word _____."

This method calls upon the power word to cue in the subconscious mind for purposes of releasing dysfunctional habits and
installing functional ones. A release statement, to be followed by
your power word, might include any one of these: "I release the
belief that I can't change," "I release my expectations of failure," "I
release my fear of change," "I release my need to criticize myself,"
or "I release my need to procrastinate."

The installation of an intention, affirmation, or new belief,
also to be followed by your power word, articulates your willingness and desire to adopt a more functional habit. A statement of
intention might be as follows: "I am willing (want, give myself
permission) to change my relationship with money." A statement
of affirmation, which presents a condition or state of being as if
it were already in existence, would be voiced as an "I am" statement, such as "I am comfortable with change." A statement of
new belief, on the other hand, would be expressed as an outcome
you are capable of achieving, such as "I can improve my financial
position." It is also possible to combine a hoped-for installation
with a release by using your power word after a release-and-
manifest statement, as in "I give up being stuck and manifest
freedom."

Any sequence you prepare to release one habit and install
another should be easy to perform and will make its effects known
inwardly. Simply repeat each statement and your power word,

adding more statements as necessary, until you note a distinct lessening of tension or overall sense of well-being. When using your power word to release a recurring uncomfortable emotion, focus on the emotion and repeat your power word until the feeling dissipates.

To overcome resistance introduced by the moving stupids, you could work with a sequence such as this:

• I release my need to feel stuck in the moving stupids. (Power word)
• I release my need for resistance. (Power word)
• I release my fear of financial change. (Power word)
• I am willing to deal with the consequences of moving forward. (Power word)
• I give myself permission to enjoy changing my financial position. (Power word)
• I can make these changes and still be safe. (Power word)
• I can make these changes and not be alone. (Power word)
• I am comfortable with change. (Power word)
• I release my resistance and manifest change. (Power word)

On the other hand, to surmount impediments introduced in response to an identity threat, you might achieve better results with this sequence:

• I release my need to maintain my current identity. (Power word)
• I release my fear of creating a new financial identity. (Power word)
• I release my fear of being unable to change my financial behaviors. (Power word)
• I want to change the way I deal with money. (Power word)
• I am willing to go through the discomforts of this change. (Power word)
• I am able to deal more comfortably with money. (Power word)

Using your power word in this way will give you a sense of control over outgrown habits that may be obstructing your financial progress. In fact, it will often diminish or eliminate the emotional charge causing the block.

Inviting your subconscious mind to participate in shifting your financial position replaces self-defeating thoughts, beliefs, emotions, and behaviors with constructive ones. As such, it serves as a potent conditioning force. Customized as needed, this method can independently eliminate barriers to progressive change and to eventual prosperity.

EXERCISE 2

Developing Financial Awareness

It requires a great deal of boldness and a great deal of caution to make a great fortune, and when you have it, it requires ten times as much skill to keep it.

—RALPH WALDO EMERSON

Serious bodybuilders often learn about the functioning of various muscle groups, the physiology of muscle mass, and the exercise equipment available for developing it. Likewise, building strong money muscles requires knowledge of the financial world, of ways to accumulate revenue, and of useful tools for money management—in short, financial awareness.

Understanding how to make, grow, and manage money provides a foundation for acquiring financial strength, defined by a consistent cash flow, surplus funds, and successful investments. But ironically, many people who yearn for this type of strength shy away from learning about finances and money management techniques. Most often their hesitation can be traced to stumbling blocks in the form of entrenched attitudes and behaviors that, once uncovered, are easily removed.

Overcoming Financial Vagueness

The most frequently occurring stumbling block is a condition I call "financial vagueness syndrome" (FVS), which is characterized by not keeping financial records, avoiding checkbook reconciliation, leaving bills unopened, bouncing checks, and spending beyond credit card limits. Symptoms of FVS include generalized fears about not having enough funds to cover checks or meet financial obligations, a perceived inability to generate surplus, perpetual wonder about where one's money has gone, and economic worries about the future.

If you routinely exhibit symptoms of FVS, understand that you probably lack established habits for dealing with money and the world of finance. Realize, too, that because individuals often correlate their value as a person with the amount of money they have, dealing with personal finances can automatically trigger unpleasant emotions. To steer clear of this type of reaction, you may be unconsciously avoiding facing the numbers associated with your finances. Worse, with public schools rarely teaching personal finance, you might be among the multitudes of people who lack familiarity with the language of money, which leads to embarrassment about asking for help.

Whatever the underlying cause for your FVS might be, recognize the temporary nature of the discomfort that accompanies unaccustomed clarity about finances. Most people I work with discover, along with their diminishing FVS, a newfound sense of safety, stability, and confidence in their ability to sustain wealth. The passing discomfort that comes from paying close attention to finances can be compared to the sore muscles that result from a new exercise program.

The Merits of Facing Resistance

Many people grappling with FVS resist developing financial awareness even while recognizing its value. The most common points of
resistance involve activities that clarify one's own financial picture,
because these activities can stimulate thoughts and emotions associated with past financial indiscretions or conditions such as low
earnings or excessive debt. Resistance also prevails among people
who, new to the world of finance, attempt to increase their knowledge of it by immersing themselves in newspapers, books, and the
media. The language of finance can be confusing and off-putting to
someone unfamiliar with its nuances. By accepting such resistance
as normal, an individual intent on increasing their financial awareness can progress rapidly toward a position of financial strength.

Naomi, at age forty-eight, knew the importance of taking
charge of her money because her friend Sheila had recently
undergone treatment for breast cancer and become financially
strapped, convincing Naomi to establish a cushion for herself.
Despite her noble intentions, however, Naomi remained oblivious
to money management procedures, including the savings and
investment options available to her through her place of employment. Soon after we began working together, she admitted that
the mere thought of looking at her money profile gave her the
"shivers," because she had made poor money decisions in the
past, including lending money to friends who never repaid her.

It did not take long for Naomi to warm up to the idea that
her resistance was a natural outgrowth of embarrassment about
earlier choices, and one she could overcome simply by becoming
more financially observant. Immediately she started keeping track
of her money. Then she asked a co-worker who read the *Wall
Street Journal* every morning at the office to let her take it home at
the end of the day. Much to her surprise, she enjoyed occasional

stories and money-management tips she found in the Personal Journal section. Sometimes she would share her excitement the next day with her co-worker, albeit a little awkwardly, paving the way to interesting discussions.

Naomi soon noticed that taking small steps into the world of finance was altering her self-concept. She saw herself as more mature and responsible and, almost effortlessly, began to spend money with more understanding of how it would impact her cash flow. Four months after we started working together, she opened a savings account into which she put 5 percent of her earnings, eventually working her way up to 10 percent. Whenever she slipped into a state of disorientation, she would refocus her attention on the goal of establishing a comfortable cushion for herself. So successful were her efforts that she not only stayed on schedule with contributions to her savings account but also managed to fly to France in time to celebrate her fiftieth birthday.

Financial Awareness and the Identity Factor

Financial awareness leads to effective outcomes because of its capacity to press a person beyond the resistance introduced by the Identity Factor and into an expanded identity. Upon becoming financially aware, an individual who previously had little comprehension of their financial position or the world of finance can begin thinking about more practical ways of handling their personal accounts or even making a foray into the world of investing. With increased awareness, a former devil-may-care attitude toward paying off debt or saving money can transform into more adult behaviors such as following a spending plan or building savings.

As these or other unfamiliar behaviors emerge, you may feel temporarily disoriented, especially when confronted by friends or family members who do not relate to your newfound knowledge and sense of fiscal responsibility. It might be tempting to respond defensively to their teasing or disrespect, or to revert to old habits for the sake of reestablishing familiar connections. Many people opt instead to avoid taking the reactions of others personally and instead seek to improve these connections.

Your relationship with money reflects your relationship with yourself. This means that an increased awareness of your personal finances mirrors a deepened understanding of how you have been treating yourself and interacting with the world around you. With this knowledge you will be equipped to make more supportive choices and move toward an increasingly fulfilling position of financial strength.

Actions

Each of these actions is designed to foster enhanced financial awareness. Introduce them gradually into your normal routine, ideally at the rate of one or two a week. Many people notice that as their awareness increases, not only do they automatically start making changes but new opportunities for growth present themselves.

1. Establish a benchmark

Use of the personal net worth form that follows (see figure 2–1) will help you establish a benchmark against which to measure your progress while developing your awareness of financial realities. To get started, photocopy the form, then enter the appropriate data and store the completed statement in your prosperity journal for future reference. As you fill in the figures, keep in mind that no one is judging you by them, except perhaps the critical voice in your head. If at first you resist determining your net worth, investigate your hesitation, using the resulting insights to overcome financial vagueness. In either event, sharing your experience of this action with a buddy can minimize discomfort.

Personal Net Worth	
Assets	
Cash on hand	$
Cash (savings)	$
Cash (checking)	$
Money market accounts	$
Certificates of deposit	$
Stocks	$
Bonds	$
Mutual funds	$
Retirement accounts	$
Clothing (market value)	$
Jewelry (market value)	$
Furniture	$
Collectibles	$
Automobiles	$
Other vehicles	$
Home or other personal residence	$
Other real estate	$
Cash value of life insurance	$
Other	$
Total Assets	$

Figure 2–1

Liabilities

Total credit card debt (from form below)	$
Mortgage on home	$
Other mortgages	$
Home equity loan	$
Automobile loan(s)	$
Other loans outstanding	$
Outstanding bills	$
Tax liability	$
Other liabilities	$
Total Liabilities	$

Credit Card Debt

Company	Account #	% Interest	Balance
			$
			$
			$
			$
			$
			$
Total Credit Card Debt			$

Total Assets – Total Liabilities = Net Worth

Total Assets	$
Total Liabilities	$
Net Worth	$

2. Define your relationship with money

Defining your relationship with money is apt to be less intimidating although equally informative. The following statements are meant to serve as a starting point. Photocopy them, check off those that apply, add any additional statements that come to mind, and date and store the completed list in your prosperity journal.

__ I am financially comfortable and invest my surplus.

__ I am financially comfortable and invest my surplus, but would like to earn more.

__ I have enough money to meet my needs and enjoy myself, but not enough to invest for the future.

__ I earn sufficient money to pay all my bills and not go into debt, but there isn't enough for extras or savings.

__ I am very careful with my money and have enough to meet my needs, but I wish I could be freer with it.

__ I am very stingy with my money and hate to spend it.

__ I earn enough to cover my current expenses but not my past obligations, such as student loans and money borrowed from friends.

__ I often spend more than I earn in a month and use credit cards to make up for the shortfall.

__ I work for myself and always fear I'll run out of money.

__ I often don't have enough money to pay my monthly bills.

__ I'm deeply in debt and can't see my way out of it.

__ I'm not earning as much as I'm capable of.

__ I don't like to pay taxes and never declare my true earnings.

__ I shop a lot and often buy things I don't need.

__ I frequently lend money to other people.

__ I lend money to people who don't pay me back.

__ I rarely balance my checkbook.

__ I'm not sure how much I owe creditors.

__ When I get the urge to buy something, I do it right away.

__ I'm ashamed of the way I deal with money.

__ I don't know enough about investing money.

__ I find the topic of financial investments very boring.

__ Money isn't important to me.

3. Keep track of your spending and earning

Begin keeping track of your money by carrying a small notebook or organizer with you and writing down everything you earn and spend, including small change such as coins for parking meters. For now, just record the description and amount of each transaction, without adding them up. Then at least three times a week, enter into your financial software all earnings, as well as all checks written and credit card charges accrued.

If you experience resistance to keeping track of your money, observe your reactions. Many people who procrastinate about getting started, for example, chastise themselves for not doing what "should" be done. If you, too, procrastinate and begin engaging in critical internal dialogue, notice your thoughts and emotions, enter them in your prosperity journal, and also share them with your prosperity buddy in order to diffuse the emotional charge.

4. Pay attention to financial news

Developing financial awareness means coming to understand not only your own financial picture but also the workings of the financial world. As tempting as it may be to zone out when you hear financial news, training yourself to pay attention to it will help you make better financial decisions. For fun, think of financial news as human interest stories in which the characters are companies, managers, employees, and customers. You could start by scanning the headlines in the business section of your local newspaper or on one or more of the Web sites listed on pages 169 and 170 at the back of this book. When you find a headline that interests you, read the article with a receptive mind. Reading national news-papers such as the *Wall Street Journal*, or magazines such as *Forbes*, *Money*, or *Business Week*, can help eliminate confusion about the financial world.

5. Learn about financial tools

To evaluate equipment for building physical muscles, you might go to a sporting goods store or a gym where you could try out various exercise machines and weights. You may also want to interview personal trainers or health club personnel to see how they might assist in your muscle-building program. The corresponding equipment needed for building money muscles can be found at banks, investment houses, schools, computer software stores, libraries, bookstores, and on the Internet. Personnel, too, are available, such as bank employees, financial advisors, credit counselors, and prosperity coaches, all of whom are equipped to guide you in sculpting, toning, and stretching your money muscles.

When you are ready to avail yourself of financial tools, remember that no prior knowledge is required. Possible options include the following:

• Speak to the customer service representative at a bank and ask about their checking accounts, savings plans, CDs, and money market funds. Find out what interest rates they offer and if any restrictions apply to the accounts, such as the number of withdrawals allowed in a specified time period. Keep in mind that the bank is like a store and you are the customer. They want to help you grow and take care of your money because that is how they make their profits.

- Determine if any schools in your area give classes in personal finance or instruction in money management software. Evaluate the offerings in relation to your immediate needs, current skill level, and interests.
- Examine computer programs designed for managing personal finances. If you own a business, evaluate professional book-keeping software. Read the information printed on the packages and consult with a knowledgeable salesperson. Speak to friends or business associates about the software they use—what they like and dislike about the programs, the learning curve they experienced after installing the software, and the quality of available technical support. When you have completed your fact-gathering, decide on the software that best meets your needs and arrange for the installation.
- At a library or bookstore peruse the financial offerings, scanning the covers and tables of contents for subjects of interest.
- On the Internet, visit sites offering financial news, calculators, free newsletters, interest-rate comparisons, investment information, and anything else of interest (see pages 169 and 170 for key site listings). Just surfing these sites can raise financial awareness.

6. Question financial messages in the media

The economies of the United States and many other developed nations depend on consumer spending. In these parts of the world, media and Internet advertisements produced by experts in psychological manipulation urge people to purchase a myriad of nonessential goods and services. Credit card companies encourage further debt by offering promotions that entice buyers to use credit rather than available funds and thus spend more money than they have.

To raise your financial awareness, approach print, broadcast, and online ads from a skeptical point of view. Looking beyond the titillating presentation, notice the words used to entice you to buy, especially if credit terms are mentioned, such as "No payments or interest for one year." The fine print in such ads usually indicates that failure to pay the entire balance within the time specified will result in interest charges on the entire amount of the purchase over the time period that was waived at the outset.

When you receive credit card offers, pay attention to the interest rates, late fees, and penalties. Attractive, low-interest-rate offers usually remain in effect for a limited time then revert to a much higher rate. Interest rates can also be raised dramatically in response to a late payment or simply at the whim of the credit card company. Be equally wary of seemingly advantageous zero-percent balance transfer offers, since credit card companies count on customers maintaining a balance long after the offer expires, at which point the companies can then charge hefty interest rates.

In addition, when shopping examine sale ads offering "Buy 1 and Get 1 for 50% Off" or "Buy 2, Get 1 Free." Translate the terms so you can understand the actual discount, which in the case of the first offer noted above is 25 percent and for the second is 33 percent. Then ask yourself if you need more than one of the same item.

7. Observe prices

Become an informed consumer and watch your budget by observing the prices you pay for things. While shopping, estimate the total amount of your purchases before arriving at the checkout station. Also relate prices to the amount of time you must work to purchase the items; to calculate this time factor, divide the price of an item by your hourly wage after taxes. Then ask yourself if it is worth your working for that amount of time in order to own the item. Gaining awareness of the value of goods and services in terms of the effort required to purchase them will help you make wiser financial decisions.

8. Order a credit report

Order a credit report (see page 170) and face the facts about your financial history. Examining your credit report can dispel fears of the unknown and enable you to take more control of your finances. For one thing, invalid postings that may negatively affect a credit rating often appear on credit reports, so if you find one on yours you can have it eliminated. For another, if your credit is less than stellar, you can explore your feelings about it, accept without shame your past financial decisions, and clean up your record so you will be able to move on with your life. Do not fall into the trap of believing that you are already in so much debt it will not matter if it gets a little worse. Such a mind-set can make it impossible to learn to trust yourself in your relationship with money.

9. Assess your resistance to financial awareness

If you are struggling with financial vagueness syndrome, consider establishing a new habit and a concept of yourself as a financially astute person, both of which take time and determination. To expand your financial identity, ask yourself these questions, keeping in mind that resistance is normal and no one is judging your rate of progress:

- How does raising my level of financial awareness threaten my concept of who I am?
- Who will I be if I let go of my financial vagueness?
- What frightens me about being financially responsible?
- How will becoming financially astute affect my position among friends and family?

10. Use your power word to move forward

Apply your power word to help release any resistance to increased financial awareness. Here are some suggested statements:
- I release my need for financial vagueness. (Power word)
- I want to be financially aware. (Power word)
- I am willing to be financially aware. (Power word)
- I give myself permission to be financially aware. (Power word)
- I release my fear of discovering my net worth. (Power word)
- I release my discomfort about facing financial numbers. (Power word)
- I am willing to look at my net worth. (Power word)
- I release my resistance to keeping track of my money. (Power word)
- I am willing to keep track of my money. (Power word)
- I keep track of my money on a daily basis. (Power word)
- I enjoy being financially aware. (Power word)

11. Reward yourself often

Reward yourself with a celebration each time you have learned something new about the world of finance. Honoring success stimulates the desire for more success and a habituation to productive behavior. Consider one of these celebrations:
- Invent your own congratulatory dance of excitement, like those used by football players after completing a touchdown.
- Indulge in a desired activity you have been putting off.
- Give yourself a day off from housework.
- Do something that is out of character for you but fulfills a secret desire.

EXERCISE 3

Identifying Financial Patterns and Underlying Emotional Themes

*If a person gets his attitude toward
money straight, it will help straighten out
almost every other area in his life.*

—BILLY GRAHAM

Before designing a bodybuilding regimen for a client, a personal trainer will take into account the person's fitness level, nutritional practices, and exercise history. Similarly, a program for financial fitness incorporates an understanding of the person's recurring financial pattern and its connection to underlying emotional themes. Invariably, individuals who identify their operative financial pattern and its underlying emotions improve their financial position.

For fifty-two-year-old Robert, who struggled to pay his bills and also save a little money, making this connection propelled him into a higher income bracket. Robert saw that his chronic lack of funds resulted from persistent feelings of deprivation, which he managed to trace to their origin. This realization sparked a desire within him to ensure that more of his needs were met, leading to a greater cash flow and sense of fulfillment.

Common Financial Patterns

Nearly every financial situation reflects one of three general patterns: seeing oneself as having less than enough, just enough, or more than enough money. The term "enough" is relative and highly individualized. For some people, having basic needs met is sufficient, engendering a sense of satisfaction and security; among others, no matter how much money they accumulate, the perception persists that they need more. Figure 3–1, on pages 58–59, illustrates these patterns and their main characteristics, as well as the accompanying thoughts, beliefs, emotions, behaviors, and relationship dynamics.

It might initially appear that people who view themselves as having less than enough money experience constant discomfort and those who see themselves as having more than enough live in joy and satisfaction. In reality, though, both financial patterns correlate with a wide range of emotional states. People who regard themselves as having less than enough money, although troubled financially, may enjoy the company of family and friends, participate in satisfying social activities, and experience success in nonfinancial areas of their life. At the same time, those who see themselves as having more than enough money might be dealing with family or work problems, feel unfulfilled creatively, suffer ongoing disappointments, or have relationship difficulties.

Still, because financial situations are created by thoughts, beliefs, and emotions, a person can enjoy more of life's bounties by changing their limiting TBEs. When this occurs, it becomes possible to advance along the continuum illustrated in figure 3–2, from a Less Than Enough to a More Than Enough financial pattern, at which point they can enrich their lives with a more rewarding set of characteristics.

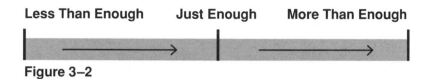

Figure 3–2

Unfortunately, most people remain in a fixed position along the first half of this continuum throughout their adult lives, confining themselves to a habitually limiting financial pattern and the traits that go with it. Even someone who advances for several years before returning to their previous position will rarely have established a new pattern.

The same can be said of individuals whose pattern is best described as shifting frequently back and forth between positions. Jim's income, for one, fluctuated in keeping with the economics of the manufacturing company he worked for. Although his base salary remained the same except for periodic cost-of-living increases, the amount of overtime he worked varied. During years with ample opportunity to work extra hours, he did, whereupon he and his wife Laura delighted in paying off debts and indulging in house repairs. Then months would follow with little available overtime, forcing Jim and Laura back into debt and misery about their lot in life. While it might appear that their income fluctuations were caused by events beyond their control, they confided to me that they had a need to express the sense of deprivation stimulated within them by Jim's up-and-down earnings. They even suspected they might have chosen this job over two others because it would allow them to act out their feelings of deprivation.

	Less Than Enough	Just Enough	More Than Enough
Features	Sense of need and lack Poor self-image A focus on the past, with worries about the future	Sense of adequacy Low self-image A focus on and concern about the future, with regrets about the past	Sense of abundance Healthy self-image A focus on the present, with positive expectations of the future
Thoughts	"I'm going to run out of money and there's no one to help me." "I wish someone would take care of me." "If only I could win the lottery." "I wonder who I can borrow money from." "I'll never get what I want." "I hate this financial struggle." "There must be something wrong with me because I can't make any money."	"If only I had a little more money, I could be comfortable." "I wish I knew how to get what I want." "I'll never have enough money to retire." "There must be something else I ought to be doing to get out of this rut."	"Life is good." "I'm doing a great job." "I like my life." "I'm grateful to be enjoying this abundance." "I'm really lucky." "I like sharing good fortune with others." "I appreciate everything I have."
Beliefs	"I'm not worthy." "There isn't enough for everyone." "There must be something wrong with me." "People like me can't make money." "I'm poor." "Money is the root of all evil." "It's not spiritual to have money." "It's noble to be poor." "If I'm poor, people will feel sorry for me."	"Wealthy people are not good." "I don't deserve luxury." "Luxury is bad." "I won't make good investment decisions, so having no surplus keeps me safe." "I'm not safe." "If I have surplus, people will want my money." "It's not safe to be wealthy." "If I'm wealthy, no one will like me." "Wealthy people don't go to heaven."	"It's an abundant world." "I have the right to have what I want." "It's OK to be rich." "Wealth is good." "I'm deserving." "I'm a good person." "I'm trustworthy." "There's enough for everyone." "Wealthy people can be kind and generous."

Figure 3–1

Emotions	Needy, empty, alone, inadequate, unworthy, unsupported, defective, unfulfilled, depressed, sense of impending doom	Frustrated, unappreciated, invisible, bored, limited, blocked	Independent, satisfied, secure, joyful, generous, proud, respected, confident, connected, appreciated, accepted, acknowledged, loved
Behaviors	Chronic debting Late bill-paying Financial vagueness Check bouncing Dreams of having lots of money Tax avoidance Obsession with financial rescue dramas	Living paycheck to paycheck Periodic debting Occasional late bill-paying Bill-paying strategizing Keeping track of money grudgingly and sporadically	Solvent Skilled at money management Charitable Generous Curious about investments Adept at making rational investment decisions
Relationship with Money	Conflicted Unstable Vague Struggling constantly Untrusting	Indifferent Vacillating	Comfortable Stable Caring Respectful Trusting
Relationships with Oneself and Others	Isolating People pleasing Having few intimate relationships Self-critical Needy Codependent Uncomfortable expressing emotions Not good at setting boundaries Untrusting Withholding Controlling or controlled	Having a small circle of friends Yearning for more people contact Fearful of taking chances socially	Socially active Well supported by friends and associates Strong interpersonal skills Adept at networking At ease with people Good at setting boundaries Self-motivated

Basic Emotional Themes

Although any emotion can be expressed through finances, in my experience most uncomfortable financial situations reflect one or more of the following: abandonment, shame, anger, deprivation, and sense of being trapped. Uncovering these emotional impulses aid in breaking habitual financial patterns, but the task is challenging. For starters, when basic themes are acted out through financial dramas, rarely are they immediately apparent; instead, a variety of related feelings may surface (see figure 3-3).

Another difficulty involved in accessing emotional themes is that they have more to do with human relationships than with money, and therefore can easily escape our notice. Fear, for instance, which seems to contribute to financial distress, is upon closer examination not about money but rather about abandonment—specifically, fear of being left alone. From this perspective, fear of running out of money correlates with fear of running out of people. And indeed, many money problems following divorce, death of a loved one, or major separation of any sort are associated with feeling left alone. Likewise, grief following the loss of loved ones is often acted out through loss of money.

All five basic emotional themes operate on a core survival level, subconsciously affecting everyone to some degree. In the case of abandonment, humans out of touch with others fail to thrive, an outcome frequently seen among neglected babies. Thus it can be said that fear of running out of money reflects not only a fear of being alone but also a fear of not surviving. This understanding accounts for the dread experienced by individuals in severe financial distress.

The Role of Emotionally Charged Childhood Experiences

The basic emotional themes underlying any financial pattern generally remain outside of adult awareness because they originate

	Acted Out As	Related Feelings

Abandonment	Lack of available funds
	Loss of job
	Frequent debting
	Loss of money through bad
	    investments
	Financial rescue dramas
	Lending of money that is not
	    repaid
	Being underpaid
	Hoarding of money or things
	Stinginess
	Check bouncing
	Victimization through a
	    financial scam
	Misfortune resulting from
	    bad financial advice
		Lonely
		Alienated
		Disconnected
		Worried about losing or
		    running out money
		Worthless
		Unsafe
		Fear of failure
		Dread
		Untrusting
		Rejected
		Disappointed
		Betrayed
		Depressed
		Sense of impending doom
		Longing

Shame	Financial vagueness Chronic debting Late bill-paying Controlling behaviors Poor investment decisions	Low self-esteem Invisible Defective Inadequate Guilty
Anger	Borrowing money without paying back Nonpayment of taxes Financial victimization Very late bill-paying Compulsive spending	Betrayed Powerless Abused Ignored Manipulated Used Frustrated
Deprivation	Compulsive shopping Overspending on clothes or household goods Pack-rat behaviors Homelessness Compulsive debting	Unloved Unappreciated Poor Isolated Empty

Sense of Being Trapped	Difficult relationships at work
	Taking on extra financial
	    burdens to help others
	Working overtime to meet
	    financial obligations
		Constrained
		Cornered
		Burdened
		Limited
		Blocked
		Unfulfilled

Figure 3 – 3

in the formative years of childhood, which most people do not readily remember. When events or relationships generate intense emotions for a child, they become "defining experiences," the effects of which linger on into adulthood and often find expression in financial dramas. Examples of defining experiences include a serious illness or accident; a sudden change in family dynamics such as divorce, death, or the birth of a new sibling; a relocation; or ongoing abuse of any kind by trusted adults or peers. Establishing the connection between a debilitating financial pattern in adulthood and a defining childhood experience stimulates a release of the emotional charge initiated in childhood, thus opening the way for a new financial pattern to emerge.

A defining moment in Tom's childhood lay at the heart of a financial situation in which he found himself at age forty-seven. Tom had a strong desire to pursue a more intellectually challenging and financially rewarding job, but kept avoiding taking action. By the time I met him, he was chronically depressed. He and his wife wanted to buy a new house, which for Tom meant finding a higher-paying job—a task that required him to get past his avoidance.

The first emotion we were able to clearly identify was a sense of impending doom that hovered over Tom and kept him from moving forward. He acknowledged that he was haunted by intense thoughts of running out of money and having no place to turn. When asked about his employment history, he said that on three occasions he had been promised a promotion then, due to company circumstances, lost his job and became strapped financially before finding a new one. Each time, his elation turned abruptly to disappointment, powerlessness, and confusion. He concluded that his current anxiety came from a sense of doom he felt because he had held his present job long enough to expect to lose it and felt powerless to stop this from happening. His hope was to find a better-paying job, but his expectation was for disaster.

When asked to remember a time in childhood marked by extreme disappointment combined with loss, Tom instantly recalled an incident that occurred at Christmas when he was six years old. He and his brother received many items they had wanted, enjoyed them for a week, then after a disagreement between his parents about money, without explanation his father returned all the presents to the store. Tom felt shocked and confused, and on a deeper level, abandoned. Upon questioning, he remembered additional incidents in which pleasant feelings transformed suddenly into a sense of abandonment.

Tom clearly saw how his Christmas experience had led him to believe that joy would be followed by disappointment and that he was powerless over the authority figures in his life. Soon after he made the connection between his current situation and his trauma at age six and expressed how abandoned he had felt at the time, his depression lifted. A few months later, he succeeded in finding a higher-paying job and purchasing the home he and his wife had wanted.

Wanda's financial predicament also reenacted a defining childhood experience. After a difficult divorce, Wanda was told by the Internal Revenue Service to make a large tax payment compensating for obligations her ex-husband had failed to meet. For five years, she battled with the IRS. Only in year six did she manage to negotiate a reasonable settlement.

After Wanda told me this story, I asked her if the IRS situation had caused her to feel bullied and picked on, and she indicated it had. I then asked who had picked on her when she was young. Wanda related how her elementary-school classmates often teased her because she was overweight and wore thick glasses. She would return home from school feeling ashamed about who she was. As she matured, Wanda lost weight and had laser eye surgery, dramatically changing her appearance, although her childhood shame remained deep within her.

When approached with the idea that she may have needed the IRS drama in order to express her shame, Wanda connected the feelings of being bullied and picked on by the IRS to the same feelings she had as a child. Had she made the connection earlier, settlement would probably have come sooner because she would have released the charge from her childhood shame and thus no longer needed a vehicle through which to express her basic emotional theme. I have worked with several clients battling difficult IRS negotiations, and once their emotions were recognized and released, the situations suddenly resolved themselves. In one instance, the IRS caseworker was replaced by a more amenable agent; in another, a new option presented itself, rapidly settling the problem.

Financial Patterns, Emotional Themes, and the Identity Factor

Financial patterns and their underlying emotional themes are so much a part of people's self-concept that any change in this groundwork is likely to activate the Identity Factor, causing great resistance. Fortunately, a person aware that their finances represent an integral part of them rather than something external, will realize the importance of creating an identity congruent with a healthy money flow, which means changing core aspects of their financial identity despite the likelihood of resistance.

To resist change at this point is akin to reinforcing a dysfunctional relationship with money. A young woman I once knew, who was unwilling to deviate from her less-than-enough financial pattern, inherited $100,000 and immediately began giving the money away in order to maintain her self-image as someone in need. If instead she had managed to hold on to the money, chances are she still would not have felt prosperous and secure unless she had changed the thoughts, beliefs, and emotions contributing to her concept of herself.

Overriding the influence of the Identity Factor effectively enough to develop a sense of yourself as prosperous can be compared to following an exercise program that gradually helps you build stronger muscles, reshape your body, and develop new relationships with people who share your interest in physical conditioning. Over time, as you cultivate the TBEs necessary to sustain your new self-image, they will come to expression in new behaviors. As a result, you will be less inclined to preserve your old position in your peer group and family of origin. With patience and discipline, you will then be able to achieve and maintain a fulfilling life position.

Actions

The actions for this exercise are intended to guide you toward the discovery of your financial pattern and its underlying emotional themes. With understanding of the scenarios you have been reenacting through your finances, you will be equipped to change inwardly and develop healthier financial habits. The first few actions involve inquiry, a long-established mode for enhancing illumination and self-reliance.

1. Identify your financial pattern

Begin identifying your predominant financial pattern by answering the following questions:

• How long have you been in your current financial situation? Would you consider it the outcome of habitual TBEs?

- If your current situation is not typical for you, what is?
- Do you tend to stay in the same financial position or does it vary from time to time? If it fluctuates, can you find an underlying pattern to the alterations?
- How much of your adult life have you spent free of debt? Have you been in debt more than out of debt?

Now, referring to figure 3-1, select the characteristics that most closely apply to you. Then decide where you are on the continuum shown in figure 3-2. Describe your primary financial pattern in your prosperity journal.

2. Recognize your basic emotional themes

Connect your financial pattern to the emotional themes holding it in place, by answering the following questions, recording each insight in your prosperity journal:

- What, if anything, is uncomfortable about your current financial situation? Name the feelings it stimulates.
- Have you been in a similar predicament in the past? If so, did it evoke the same feelings you are experiencing now?
- Can you recall having had these uncomfortable feelings as a child? If so, describe the circumstances.
- Did you experience other defining moments in the past, especially events involving loss or separation? Do any of these moments relate to feelings stirred up by your current financial situation?
- Does anyone involved in your current financial situation remind you of your parents, siblings, or other influential childhood figures? Can you relate your present feelings to the unpleasant feelings you harbored toward these individuals?
- Using figure 3–3, determine the emotional themes that give rise to the cluster of feelings most familiar to you.

3. Relate your financial pattern and emotional themes to your identity

To understand how changes in the pattern and theme representing your financial position can undermine your progress by leading to resistance, answer the following questions:

- If you were to improve your financial position, what aspects of it would feel unfamiliar to you?
- If your income were to increase significantly, what concerns might you have about managing the surplus?
- If you were to significantly increase your income and develop skills for handling it, how might this impact your relationships with your peers, your family of origin, and your significant other?
- How would prosperity affect decisions about where you live and work? Would a change in either location require you to separate from people you enjoy being with? How would you feel about such a separation?

4. Expand your financial identity

Knowing what you do about the financial pattern and underlying emotional themes governing your use of money, add to the definition of your financial identity that you recorded in your prosperity journal. First, identify your financial pattern (Less Than Enough, Just Enough, More Than Enough) and list the emotions you habitually act out through your use of money. Second, define your financial position with respect to your friends and family (Do you earn less than they do, about the same amount, or more?) and the emotions this routinely generates within you. Conclude by proposing ways in which your self-concept is likely to expand beyond the expectations of peers and family, and how to support the expansion you might go about realigning these relationships.

5. Notice resistance or disorientation resulting from change

An instinctual need to protect your old identity can spark active resistance to moving forward, in the form of procrastination, avoidance, forgetfulness, or annoyance. If you are a victim of financial vagueness syndrome, you may feel suddenly disoriented. Whatever your symptoms happen to be as you begin to progress, share them with your prosperity buddy, who can then remind you that they are temporary and the natural consequences of building your money muscles and improving your relationship with money.

EXERCISE 4

Setting Attainable Goals

If your only goal is to become rich,
you will never achieve it.
—JOHN D. ROCKEFELLER

Only if given a client's specific performance goals can a personal trainer develop a bodybuilding regimen for achieving them. In the same way, the formulation of well-thought-out financial goals helps the person launch strategies for attaining them.

To be attainable, financial goals require, first and foremost, a description that is time-sensitive enough to guide money-related behaviors. A goal of eliminating credit card debt of $15,000 *within one year*, for example, would ideally motivate you during that circumscribed period of time to buy only items you can pay for out of available funds. Thus, when confronted with the opportunity to buy something on credit at an attractive price, you would refuse. Likewise, a goal of doubling your income in two years might provide incentive for cultivating investments, starting a part-time business, or expanding a current one. The formulation of goals that can actually be achieved requires more subliminal considerations as well.

Personal Values

Basing your goals on outcomes that deeply matter to you increases your chances of attaining these objectives because of the feelings of fulfillment they inspire within you each step of the way. In addition, when you climb a financial ladder of your own creation—rather than one imported from your partner, friends, neighbors, or family—your success hinges not only how much money you have accumulated but on how many of your dreams have come to fruition.

To move in this direction, it is a good idea to become keenly aware of your values concerning health, lifestyle, relationships, employment, education, and humankind's collective well-being. Do you prize simplicity, for instance, or spending time with loved ones, or volunteering at a local charity? Without knowing your innermost values, the pursuit of your material aspirations may eclipse your happiness by requiring you to inadvertently sacrifice these nonmaterial desires. Prioritizing your values and basing your income goals on those you consider nonnegotiable increases your chances of satisfying both your internal and external needs as you advance financially.

At age thirty-five, while evaluating a management position with a Fortune 500 company, Louise learned the importance of taking her personal values into account—and not a moment too soon. Having moved up the corporate rungs for eight years, she was tempted to accept the $200,000-a-year offer; but suddenly it dawned on her that carrying out the job responsibilities and expectations of her supervisor would force her to delay childbearing and, due to high stress levels, possibly jeopardize her health. Knowing the job conflicted significantly with her values, Louise had no difficulty declining the promotion.

Don, on the other hand, at age twenty-six and single, was highly motivated to accrue a net worth of a million dollars within five years and consequently jumped at the chance to manufacture specialized surfboards in partnership with his friend Steve. Everything about the venture appealed to him: working with Steve's designs, selling and marketing, the people in the industry, the challenge of starting a business from scratch, and most of all, surfboarding itself. The undertaking meshed perfectly with his personal values, and within five years Don did indeed reach his financial goal, after which he set new goals that took into account the values he shared with his wife of three years.

Whereas the respect for personal values keeps people on course while pursuing material goals, ignoring these values generally leads to self-abandonment. In such instances, financial behaviors show up in the form of repeated losses associated with compulsive spending, chronic debting, frequent lending, or poor investments—all the more reason for prioritizing values while formulating your financial goals.

Realistic Financial Objectives

Effective goal-setting also requires a healthy dose of realism in order to override the impulses of the subconscious mind. On its own, a subconscious mind accustomed to protecting personal identity and maintaining a less-than-enough or just-enough financial pattern, will set its sights on an amount of money so far beyond practicality that no concrete plan for moving forward can possibly develop. Worse, the resulting inaction tends to reinforce the emotional theme of deprivation, locking the person into a cycle of dysfunction. To counteract the likelihood of such an occurrence and foster instead the development of a viable plan of action, it is essential to establish objectives that are realistic.

Brenda found this out on her own. A life coach who used credit cards whenever she needed supplies or equipment for her business, Brenda spoke jokingly of solving her financial problems by someday winning the lottery. She hated the $10,000 she perennially owed on her credit cards, wanted to buy a home of her own, and yearned for more fashionable clothes, but rarely did she earn more than $35,000 a year. While attending a group I facilitated, she quickly recognized the thread of deprivation weaving throughout her life. She also came to understand that getting what she wanted was frightening, because satisfaction was out of character for her.

After recognizing that she was protecting her identity by entertaining fantasies of sudden wealth, Brenda began to set attainable income goals based on realistic objectives that were time specific. First, she determined to strive for monthly earnings of $3,200, an increase of 10 percent, or about $300, over her previous earnings. To reach this goal, she needed four additional client sessions a month—a prospect so feasible she eagerly began networking to draw in more clients. She also agreed to keep track of her spending and not use her credit cards. Within four weeks, Brenda had three new clients; and by the end of another two weeks she had reached her goal and begun to set a new one. The increase in her income helped her pay off her credit card debt and was gradual enough for her to adapt fluidly to the new cash flow.

Setting realistic goals for debt reduction can happen in other ways as well. If, unlike Brenda, you expect your income to remain steady, your goal may be to curtail spending, in which case you will need to delineate where to cut back and how much money to allocate to debt repayment. Just facing your debt is likely to present possibilities, such as negotiating for lower interest on credit cards or working with a reputable credit counselor. In the end you may decide to bring in extra money through a part-time job. With an honest intention to reduce your debt and a series of realistic goals in place, there is little to stop you from attaining them. The same can be said of an intention to increase your income, enhance your savings, augment your investments, or purchase a new home.

Consequences

Too often, people who desire significant sums of money imagine that their problems will all be solved when the funds arrive, giving little thought to the consequences of acquiring the funds or having them in their possession. The fact is that nearly any method chosen to increase cash flow will also initiate lifestyle alterations that may or may not be desirable. Changing jobs, for instance, might require relocation, and modifying business protocols may necessitate working longer hours or hiring more personnel requiring supervision. Similarly, moving into a larger home in a new neighborhood, while fulfilling a dream, could engender feelings of isolation or disconnectedness from social supports.

An inflow of funds also requires multiple money-management decisions involving how the revenue will be allocated, what will be done with the surplus, and who will administer it. Even with incremental increases in earned income, each rung of the financial ladder can present concerns requiring individualized attention. A person who does not enjoy this type of activity may decide at some point to stop climbing and savor what they have.

In looking toward the future, you might cringe at the idea of spending hours each day caring for or even thinking about excessive sums of money. Instead of great wealth, what you may actually long for could be peace of mind, a sense of security, or job satisfaction—all of which are emotional states, not financial objectives. In either case, by extending your focus to include emotional and other internal consequences, you are more likely to set goals you can remain faithful to and take pleasure in pursuing.

Long- and Short-Term Goals

Effective strategies inspiring ongoing dedication are usually composed of two tiers: long-term goals delineating the big picture of hoped-for achievements and short-term goals outlining intermediary steps that allow for the experience of frequent success. If, for example, a long-term goal involves amassing a surplus of funds, saving a small sum on a weekly basis can potentially stimulate constructive thoughts about the endeavor while dissolving long-held feelings of shame or deprivation. As thoughts and emotions shift, so does the corresponding financial position, opening a pathway to prosperity fueled by internal achievements.

Long-term goals are most likely to bear fruit when given a time parameter and considerable detail. Many people, when asked what they want to achieve financially, answer with statements like "I want enough money to be free to do whatever I wish" or "I never want to worry about money again." But such vague hopes fail to foster the development of a strategy leading to measurable achievement. By contrast, the more specific you are about your income-producing plans, the better prepared you will be to cultivate the skills needed to accomplish them. If, for instance, you set your sights on increasing your net worth to $1,000,000 through real estate investments over the course of five years, you could plan to spend a portion of the first year talking to seasoned investors, reading books or attending seminars about real estate, investigating the local real estate market, considering potential properties, or perhaps becoming a real estate agent. Each of these activities, while propelling you toward your goal, would also help you decide if real estate investing aligns with your values.

When determining long-term goals it is better to be specific not only in terms of what you want materially but also with regard to perceptions you would like to have about yourself and your life.

Long-term goals would therefore include big dreams regarding income, net worth, and lifestyle, as well as desired feeling states such as secure, satisfied, respected, and joyful—factors often ignored when devising a financial plan.

Short-term goals, on the other hand, inspire momentum when depicted in measurable terms and allowed to unfold within three months to a year. A three-month goal might involve raising client fees by a specific amount, as well as learning a financial software program, keeping track of spending on a daily basis, or doing research that supports one of your long-term goals. A one-year goal could focus on increasing your customer base by 20 percent, paying down debt by 50 percent, or raising your yearly income by 25 percent. Attaining a series of short-term goals establishes a pattern of success that can override a habitual tendency toward procrastination, avoidance, or failure, and program your subconscious to expect positive outcomes.

When devising short-term goals, also focus on desired internal states. If, for example, peace of mind is one of your long-term goals, then a short-term goal might include reducing stress by taking a weekly yoga class, meditating 20 minutes a day, or spending at least an hour each week outdoors in a natural setting. Peace of mind could also be supported by asking for a raise, counteracting financial vagueness, or developing a plan for limiting your spending.

To keep your short- and long-term goals congruent with your personal values, reevaluate your goals frequently and adjust them when necessary. After a series of short-term successes, you may find a long-term financial goal of earning millions of dollars, for example, had been sparked by feelings of abandonment, shame, or deprivation that are no longer a part of your internal environment. Or you might link it to a nonproductive thought pattern such as comparing your income to the fortunes of others or to your need for parental respect. In either instance, this would be the time to invite new goals to emerge from your more evolved perception of yourself and your life.

Now, instead of great financial wealth you might prefer a deepened, more loving relationship with yourself and your family. Fulfilling a goal of this sort can result in a better-integrated outcome, such as a pattern of having more-than-enough material goods combined with feelings of freedom and accomplishment. At this point, you can perceive yourself as wealthy without having to amass large sums of money or material goods. And you will be able to evaluate, from a more comfortable place, just how far you want to go financially and why.

When adjusted as needed, a two-tiered strategy for fulfilling attainable goals becomes self-perpetuating by stimulating notice-able shifts both internally and externally. Just the recording of your daily spending and earning, for instance, can improve your self-image, making you more amenable to trying another new financial behavior. This in turn can generate increased self-trust, drawing into your life opportunities that are in tune with your new state of being and, as illustrated in figure 4-1, activating a cycle of change.

When Your Goals Transcend Your Financial Identity

Setting goals capable of propelling you into an improved financial position can conceivably reinforce dysfunctional behaviors. For one thing, such goals may stimulate latent fears of failure. For another, if you identify more with failure than success, negative expectations might prevent you from developing a feasible strategy for implementing your goals. Third, anxiety about losing your position among your peers or family can provide fodder for avoiding goal-oriented actions.

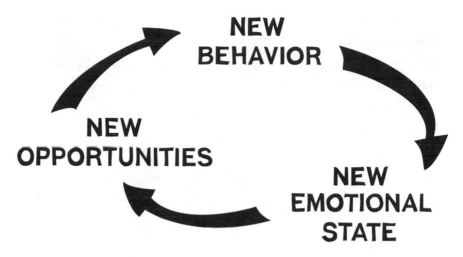

Figure 4–1 What new behavior might you adopt to initiate a cycle of change?

The more willing you are to recognize these possibilities and accept such behavior as normal, the less likely you will be to criticize yourself and consequently block your forward momentum. The solution, then, is to support your long-term progress through a series of realistic short-term goals that can help you adapt to gradual changes in your financial position while moving through the disorientation that is likely to occur. This gradual movement, compared with pursuing dreams of mushrooming wealth, results in a greater degree of comfort and the potential for more lasting results.

Actions

1. Examine your values

To increase your likelihood of establishing attainable goals, examine the twenty values most important to you. Write down each one in your prosperity journal, introducing it in a statement beginning with "It is important to me that _____" or "I value _____," such as:

- It is important to me that I spend at least an hour a day with my children.
- It is important to me that I work for someone who appreciates my talents.
- It is important to me that I succeed as an entrepreneur.
- It is important to me to work at a place that provides health insurance.
- It is important to me to find an ongoing source of residual income.
- I value truth.
- I value compassion.
- I value reliability.
- I value my privacy.
- I value my relationship with my partner (spouse, child).
- I value my relationship with my house of worship (my religion, a higher power).
- I value a peaceful work environment.
- I value getting paid a fair wage for the work I do.

From the list you have compiled, choose five statements that are nonnegotiable. Consider the selected statements reflections of values on which you will not renege, no matter how dire the circumstances might appear.

2. Outline your long-term goals

Create a form like the one that follows, entering in the right-hand column the goals you hope to achieve over the next five to ten years. Be as specific as possible.

This form distinguishes net worth from yearly income to help you give each one the attention it deserves. Your net worth goal will be more comprehensive since it takes into account available cash, the value of your possessions, and your debt. If your goal is to be a millionaire, you will need a net worth of one million dollars,

To fulfill my big dreams, at the end of 7 years I will have:	
My dream house	A 3,500-square-foot multilevel house in the hills of Boulder, Colorado, with a family living room containing a large television, an office for my wife, a study where I can work on occasion and practice my clarinet, and a kitchen with a center island
My live-in companion(s)	My wife and our two teenagers
My sources of income	My printing business located in downtown Boulder, real estate investments, and my wife's Internet firm
My yearly income	$300,000
My net worth	$1.4 million
My social circle	A few close friends and a wide array of acquaintances
My leisure-time activities	Skiing with the family, playing the clarinet, reading, and visiting with friends
My feelings about life	A sense of comfort, acceptance and respect professionally, financial security, satisfaction with my work and marriage, and appreciation for the time spent with my wife and my children

Figure 4–2

not an income of that amount. Keep in mind that your net worth can increase in response to wise investments, debt repayment, increased savings, or the acquisition of costly possessions.

To evaluate your long-term goals with respect to your personal values and your current identity, ask yourself the following questions:

• Are my goals in tune with my personal values?
• Are my goals congruent with my current financial identity? If they aren't, am I willing to change? What alterations can I agree to make?

• How might my attainment of these goals affect my relationships with friends and family? Am I willing to experience such consequences? How might I avoid negative consequences associated with achieving these goals?

3. Set short-term lifestyle goals

In order to move toward achieving your long-term goals, establish shorter-term objectives based on your answers to the following questions:
• What steps do I have to take to achieve my long-term nonfinancial goals?
• What do I have to learn in order to take these steps?
• Which of these goals am I willing to commit to over the next three months?
• Which ones am I willing to dedicate myself to over the next twelve months?

4. Establish one-year financial goals

In your prosperity journal, record measurable one-year goals that can move you closer to your long-term income and net-worth goals, making sure to update them at the end of each year as needed. For instance, if your long-term goal is to quadruple your net worth within seven years, your one-year goal might be to increase your net worth by 20 percent; over each of the subsequent six years, plan on enlarging the percentage of increase.

Include in your one-year financial goals specific methods for increasing both your income and your net worth. Possible income-enhancing methods include salary hikes, greater business profits, and higher-yield investments. Net worth expansion could come from appreciation in the value of your house or other material goods, increased savings or value of investments, or debt reduction.

Read over your one-year goals at least once a month, rekindling your dedication to them. These reviews will help keep your creative thinking on track.

5. Test-market your financial goals

To ensure that your financial goals are realistic and aligned with your personal values, act as if you have attained them and then investigate your options. While exploring your alternatives for surplus funds, for instance, imagine that you have $10,000 and begin reading about investment possibilities. As you do, revise your objectives, replacing any misinformation with valuable facts.

Next, practice making investments. If you are interested in the stock market, select a stock and begin "paper trading," deciding how many shares you will buy at what price, following the stock, and eventually deciding when to sell it. Once your profits exceed your losses, consider actually investing in a few stocks.

Likewise, shopping for houses in an unfamiliar price bracket can help hone your purchasing intentions. If you think you want to live in a specific neighborhood, attend open houses that meet your criteria and imagine yourself actually living in them. Ask yourself practical questions: Would I enjoy taking care of a house this size? What new furnishings would I have to get? Does the neighborhood meet my safety requirements? How will living here affect my children? Your answers to such questions may convince you to revise your lifestyle goals.

6. Devise a strategy for reaching your financial goals

Common strategies for generating income include trading time for money, as in a job or your own service-oriented business; buying goods and selling them at a profit; and establishing sources of residual income such as investments, royalties from books, and revenue from rental properties. One or more of these strategies can be adopted to increase your earnings. If you have a job, for instance, you could request a raise, improve your position within the company, or find a better job. Or you could supplement your job income by buying and selling products or building residual income. Other methods can be adopted for goals pertaining to debt reduction or increased savings. Whichever approach you choose, make sure it coincides with your personal values and will help you move toward your lifestyle goals as well.

After deciding on a strategy, note any new skills or information you will need to implement it. Then incorporate all necessary prerequisites into your overall plan.

7. Prepare to adjust your goals

Set your goals with the understanding that you will probably need to adjust them in response to changed internal or external circumstances that emerge. At such times, plan to clarify your thinking by sharing your concerns with either your prosperity buddy or someone close to you.

8. Visualize reaching your goals

Through visualization, you can increase your receptivity to new opportunities that come your way. The most effective visualizations include mental images and corresponding emotional states. Here is a helpful technique:

• Sit in a chair with your back as straight as possible, feet either crossed at the ankles or flat on the floor, and hands resting gently on your lap. To focus your attention, take a few deep breaths, observing your chest and abdomen as you inhale and exhale. If your mind is very active, simply observe it without judgment as you continue to breathe deeply.

- When you feel relaxed, let your breathing return to normal and imagine that you have accomplished one of your long-term financial or lifestyle goals. See yourself in this state of mastery, enjoying your success and sharing your satisfaction, joy, or pride with others. Sit with this image and feeling for several minutes.
- Next, silently repeat affirmations followed by your power word, such as "I have reached my goal" (power word), "I live in the house of my dreams" (power word), "My business grosses $_____ per month" (power word), or "I am solvent and have more than enough money" (power word). Continue to imagine the experience of reaching your goal, including the feeling states you hope to achieve. Enhance the image in whatever way you wish, perhaps by picturing the people with whom you intend to share the results of your efforts. If your mind wanders, gently bring it back to this focal point, savoring the feelings of success. If fear or anxiety arises, repeat your power word until the counterproductive feeling dissipates.
- Sit with the image and related feelings for as long as you wish. When you are ready, gently return your attention to your body, take a deep breath, and open your eyes.

9. Release discomfort about moving forward slowly

Become aware of any discomfort you may have about proceeding at a gentle pace. Keep in mind that mentally accepting only a large shift in income, with the corresponding possibility of either quickly paying off debts or rapidly fulfilling material desires, can impede progress. If you have significant debt, do your best to override motivations stemming from a desire for instant gratification. In times of debt, becoming solvent will most likely require patience and an understanding of the emotions driving your need to have more than you can afford.

Any time you notice discomfort about a slower-than-hoped-for pace, repeat appropriate statements with your power word, such as:
- I am willing to slow down in order to move forward. (Power word)
- I release my resistance to developing a functional strategy. (Power word)
- I want to develop a functional strategy. (Power word)
- I give myself permission to develop a functional strategy. (Power word)
- I have a functional strategy. (Power word)
- I am willing to adjust my expectations. (Power word)
- I release my fear of making changes. (Power word)
- I am willing to use cash or checks instead of credit cards. (Power word)
- I have enough money to buy what I need. (Power word)
- I release my fear of solvency. (Power word)
- I want to be solvent. (Power word)
- I am solvent. (Power word)
- I easily and consistently earn _____ dollars a month. (Power word)

PART II

Toward
a New
Financial
Identity

INTRODUCTION

S haped by our thoughts, beliefs, emotions, behaviors, and relationships concerning money, our financial identity is an aspect
of our personality. When the personality shifts, the financial identity, a determinant of our financial health, also changes. Inter-
esingly, studies have shown that when patients with dissociative
identity disorder (DID) or multiple personality disorder (MPD)
switch personalities, they exhibit a corresponding transformation
in their physiology. Candace Pert, Ph.D., a neuroscientist and
author of *Molecules of Emotion*, said on a CD entitled *Your Body Is
Your Subconscious Mind*, "People literally have different bodies
when they have different personali[ties]."

   After first reading about this phenomenon in the early 1980s,
when I had both physical disorders and financial problems, I sensed
the interconnection between the mind, body, and financial health,
concluding that to become healthy physically, emotionally, and
financially, I had to "switch" personalities, replacing my sick,
needy, financially dysfunctional personality with one that was

healthy, strong, and able to generate prosperity. I have no doubt the resulting transformation contributed to my subsequently improved financial circumstances.

To begin transforming your personality to achieve financial health, it may help to understand that everyone has a variety of personalities that they exhibit in different situations, such as at work, meetings, or while gathering with friends or family. In fact, according to Frank W. Putnam, M.D., author of *Diagnosis and Treatment of Multiple Personality Disorder*, people with MPD differ from healthy individuals only in terms of degree: they dissociate to a greater extent between personalities and have fewer cross memories.

To further comprehend how different personalities may affect financial health, visualize your body as a boardinghouse lodging a cast of characters that might include a wounded inner child seeking solace, a critical parent determined to undermine the child's self-confidence, a rebellious teenager without financial responsibility, and a wise adult who understands what the boardinghouse needs to function effectively and who manages money successfully, as shown in figure II–1. Each character plays an important role in the workings of the boardinghouse and takes charge periodically: in family relationships, the one at the helm may be the critical parent; in the workplace, the rebellious teenager; and in challenging circumstances, the wounded child. Ideally, the wise adult maintains authority in situations relating to money management, although for many people this character sits quietly in the background while the others act out their roles, resulting in financial problems.

Often, for example, the wounded child, rebellious teenager, or critical parent controls behavior, leading to feelings of discomfort, excessive debting, underearning, lack of record keeping, compulsive shopping, refusal to pay taxes, or chronic late payment of bills.

Figure II–1 Who lives in your boardinghouse?

The wise adult may watch the drama until the others ask for help, expressing their commitment, at which point the wise adult can more readily coordinate a team to foster healthy financial behaviors.

To forge a financial identity characterized by responsible money management, it is essential to acknowledge and support the wise adult within you who often waits for a conscious commitment from other players before assuming authority. While turning control over to this character, you can also use techniques to satisfy and comfort the other characters vying for attention, so they will no longer feel the need to assert their power. Then all the characters, primed to work together, will be able to help you progress to more fulfilling life circumstances.

By encouraging the wise adult to take charge, a person can significantly change their behavior, transforming themselves from a dependent, underearning debtor, for example, to an individual exhibiting self-reliance and financial independence. And because of the orchestration involved, such a metamorphosis does not result in a rapid personality shift as in DID, but rather unfolds gradually, over an extended period of time, like the square morphing into the circle shown in figure II–2.

Figure II–2 How slowly are you willing to shift your personality to achieve financial health?

While moving consciously through a significant transformation, people notice subtle changes occurring almost daily. A slight positive shift in attitude, for instance, might lead to a new thought that stimulates a more comfortable emotion and functional behavior, all of which can catalyze minor yet observable improvements in life circumstances. Over time, such incremental upgrades can amount to a major modification in life position. The same holds true in financial growth.

Approaching change less consciously, on the other hand, can easily lead to stagnation. Many people who seek to quickly change their financial position, altering a few financial behaviors in the hope of rapidly accumulating wealth, feel discouraged when only a minor change in their financial situation occurs. And when a rapid change actually does arise, such as the unexpected infusion of a large sum of money, it tends to provoke disruption in the "boardinghouse" until internal and external adjustments are made, generally over an extended period of time. For this reason, remaining aware of subtleties and understanding that you are morphing, not vaulting, into a new financial position can make the process more satisfying and enjoyable.

Individuals who adopt a holistic approach as they gradually make minor alterations to elements of their financial identity permanently improve their relationship with money. Occasional relapses are to be expected despite great determination, however, because aspects of an established identity can be strong enough to hinder progress. For example Denise, a fifty-year-old self-demeaning business owner whose financial pattern was to have just enough money, made sufficient changes in her financial identity to be able to put aside $10,000 and continue saving several hundred dollars a month. After proudly maintaining this surplus for over a year, she became secure in thinking of herself as having more than enough money and thus decided to expand her business. But no sooner did new profits start flowing in than Denise, unaccustomed to managing so much money and now exceedingly busy, fell behind in her financial record-keeping. Six months after beginning the expansion, she realized she had bought far too much office equipment on credit and owed almost as much as she had saved. Once again she was back to her familiar pattern of having just enough money.

Because of her holistic perspective, Denise was able to analyze the situation without reverting to her old habit of degrading herself. In the process, she discovered she had been harboring fears about the effect of wealth on her lifestyle, which had most likely prompted the relapse into her old financial pattern. As a result, she came to see that developing a new financial identity can include taking some backward steps in the interest of integrated growth. Within a few months, Denise was back on track, with the understanding that paying attention to her money was essential for developing a healthy financial identity.

To minimize the effect of the Identity Factor as you work through the five exercises in Part II, you will be gradually and consciously replacing the thoughts, beliefs, emotions, and behaviors that support your current financial identity. Just as a bodybuilding regimen includes specific exercises for individual muscles such as biceps, triceps, and deltoids, this program for building money muscles requires altering TBEs and financial behaviors to advance toward a secure and comfortable future. And just as several physical muscles move simultaneously during an exercise routine, TBEs operate as a unit to influence financial behavior (see figure II-3). As a result, altering one will automatically affect the others and change the dynamics of your financial situation.

For a glimpse into the interrelatedness of TBEs and its effect on financial behavior, consider the simple act of paying a credit card bill. The thought "I need to pay this bill," when accompanied by the belief "Not paying this bill can hurt my credit rating"

Figure II–3 How do your TBEs interact to invigorate a finacial behavior?

combined with fear of the consequences of nonpayment, stimulates a behavior—paying the bill.

Although TBE elements are interconnected, looking at them individually, as in Exercises 5, 6, and 7, provides less complex and more concrete avenues for change. Because for most people thoughts are easier to recognize than beliefs or emotions, this section of the book proceeds from replacing limiting thoughts to working on beliefs and emotions before examining financial behaviors and the relationships reflected through your finances. In reality, however, the actions for these exercises are as effective when performed in any order whatsoever.

Finally, moving toward a new financial identity by focusing on financial thoughts, beliefs, and emotions would be meaning- less without an understanding of personal TBEs. Because financial relationships reflect relationships with oneself, some actions in this section involve TBEs about the self and corresponding behaviors.

EXERCISE 5

Replacing Unproductive Financial Thoughts

*You must become a financial success in your thinking
long before you achieve it in your reality*
—Brian Tracey

Although bodybuilding routines emphasize physical exercises for specific muscle groups, the attitude of athletes also contributes to their ultimate success. Frequent self-encouragement, expectations of positive results, and a willingness to follow their trainer's instructions all drive a bodybuilder's progress. Similarly, any program designed to build money muscles must include the development of positive thoughts about oneself and money that contribute to well-being and attainment of financial goals.

The need for replacing unproductive financial thoughts becomes evident as soon as one accepts the idea that a person's thoughts, beliefs, and emotions create their reality. It then becomes apparent how negative self-talk contributes to underearning, financial loss, or chronic debting. Most often such negativity is coupled with worry about potential losses or about dire consequences resulting from insufficient funds. But when the mind is filled instead with positive and expansive thoughts, it becomes possible, according to this premise, to generate substantial financial resources.

It's Never about Money

Behind any internal dialogue about finances lie deeper issues concerning our relationships with self and others. Developing thoughts that translate into an improved relationship with money therefore requires some understanding of what your current financial thoughts actually represent. A good way to discover the real issues being expressed through your thoughts about money is by interrupting them with the phrase "It's never about money and always about my relationship with myself and others," then examining what your money problems in fact reflect.

Donna, for example, frequently complained that her husband Bob's financial irresponsibility was putting a lot of pressure on her and causing her to worry that if something happened to either of them, there would be insufficient resources to cover medical bills or even day-to-day expenses. After pointing out to Donna that the money was not the problem, I asked her to tell me what she was really concerned about. She explained that she and Bob had no one to turn to for help and she was afraid of being in trouble and all alone. Upon further questioning, she recalled that when she was in elementary school, both her parents worked and insisted she come home immediately after school every day. Since they were not friendly with their neighbors, Donna, an only child, wondered what she would do if something happened to her while she was alone. And indeed, minor crises did occasionally arise, frightening her for days afterward.

Donna also realized that she was angry with Bob for not being more supportive emotionally, and she saw that thinking about their financial situation was safer than expressing her anger or asking him to be more empathic, which might only scare him away. Her concerns about money, she concluded, were really about being left alone. Before long, Donna began practicing techniques for releasing anger and deepening her relationships with others, which decreased her mental turbulence.

At the same time, she and Bob learned to communicate their true concerns, eliminating much of the tension between them. And the more honest they became with each other, the less they focused on financial issues. Soon, instead of bickering about potential money problems, they started investigating income-producing strategies. In the process, Donna and Bob both came to understand that their fixations on financial catastrophe had masked underlying emotional needs—an awareness that helped them approach their finances with shared vision.

Whose Voice Are You Hearing?

Since our relationship with money reflects in part our relationship with ourselves, the nature of our self-talk can affect our financial situation. Consequently, it is important to determine the origins and viewpoints of your internal voices. Viewing yourself as a boardinghouse, realize that each of the personalities living inside you has its own voice expressed as thoughts. When you get dressed in the morning, for example, the critical parent might say to you, "Your clothes look awful and your hair is a mess. People are going to think you're a real dork." The wounded child might chime in with, "I never have enough money to buy new clothes." Or the rebellious teenager might growl, "I don't care what I look like or what others think." The wise adult, on the other hand, would most likely say, "Your clothes look fine just the way they are, and anyway it's your inner life that is most important."

Because your TBEs create your reality, it follows that the chorus of internal voices habitually playing out their drama in your head determines the thoughts you entertain about yourself and about money. A positive tone fosters an enjoyable life experience and a comfortable financial position, while a negative one helps bring about the opposite effect. Fortunately, if negative thinking has become a habit, with determination it can be replaced.

Changing the nature of your self-talk can lead to improved relationships and a new financial position. For example, replacing the critical parent in your head with a nurturing mother or father who often praises and encourages you is likely to help you establish a loving, supportive relationship with yourself that will be reflected physically, emotionally, and financially.

Developing New Thinking Habits

Replacing thoughts that keep you stuck financially with thoughts that lead to increased prosperity requires vigilance and a dedication to developing new thinking habits. Vigilance begins by noticing the tone of your internal dialogue and how it may be hindering your financial progress. Using figure 5-1, familiarize yourself with the differences in tone that distinguish productive thoughts from unproductive ones; then relate these to your own thinking habits. Each time you notice yourself indulging in an unproductive thought, consider how it might be impacting your finances. Perhaps you habitually rehash memories of being emotionally unsupported by your family. This type of thinking can translate into underearning or chronic debting. Once you become aware of such unproductive thinking, you can choose to focus on the present instead of the past and to notice the support you do receive from others, thus generating thoughts with a positive tone.

Unproductive Thoughts	Productive Thoughts
Worries about the future	Hope for the future
Regrets about the past	Acceptance of the past
Use of negative words, such as *can't* and *won't*	Use of affirming, positive words, such as *can* and *will*
Attachment to old methods	Openness to new possibilities
Contemplations of victimhood	Expectations for improving your circumstances
Disregard for yourself or your abilities	Confidence in yourself and your abilities
Anticipations of lack	Appreciation for what you have
Disrespect for your accomplishments	Respect for your accomplishments
Self-criticism	Self-praise

Figure 5–1

Worries about the future heads the list of unproductive thoughts and typifies the thinking of people knee-deep in financial problems. This kind of thinking is particularly inhibiting because it casts negative attention on conditions that do not exist, potentially contributing to their manifestation. Similarly, regrets about past behaviors or circumstances impede progress because they direct attention to old wounds and thereby possibly reinforce old states of being. Assuming prosperous outcomes without regretting the past or worrying about the future produces more functional behaviors. And for most people, developing such a positive outlook takes considerable practice.

Quieting the Mind

The greatest challenge to altering habitual thought patterns comes from the nature of an untrained mind, which tends to jump from one focal point to another as multiple voices in the boardinghouse vie for attention. To function effectively as a team, the entire cast of internal characters must make a group decision to heed the guidance of the wise adult, the part that knows the individual's purpose and how to fulfill it.

Certain characters within you may clamor for instant wealth, for example, while the wise adult, knowing this would not be in your best interest, might guide you to a plan for increasing your income that honors your values and cultivates your creative expression. At the same time, you might feel prodded to increase your financial awareness and employ money management techniques, both of which would give you greater ability to handle more income. But all this guidance can only be heard if you listen for it with a quiet mind.

Altered Thoughts and the Identity Factor

Only resistance to having a personality characterized by joy and satisfaction can block the shift from negative to positive thinking. Despite the dreams people have of experiencing satisfaction and joy on a daily basis, when they begin to attain such personality traits they often tend to resist it and revert to old thought patterns because they have not established routines for responding to consistently positive outcomes. In fact, frequently feeling good, a side effect of positive thinking, can confuse individuals who derive a certain amount of comfort from familiar states of distress.

In addition to gravitating toward the comfort of familiar states, newcomers to altered habits of thinking are also influenced by prior expectations. When life seems to go smoothly for weeks at a time, for instance, those accustomed to periodic difficulties tend to expect the occurrence of something unpleasant—an unproductive thought that can very well influence reality. Fortunately, awareness of these types of resistance can keep positive thinking on track.

Actions

The actions for this exercise can help you increase awareness of your current thought patterns by learning how to quiet your mind and develop focus. They also provide assistance in establishing new, more productive thoughts that lead to a more functional financial identity capable of promoting prosperity.

1. Set an intention to listen to your thoughts

Changing your internal dialogue and allowing a new financial identity to emerge begins with developing an awareness of your current thoughts about money, especially those that cause discomfort. If you haven't already developed the habit of paying attention to your thoughts, especially about money, make a statement of intention such as "I am willing to pay attention to the nature of my thoughts." To develop the habit of focusing on your thoughts, place notes with this statement of intention around your house, including one next to your bed to be read each morning. In addition, share your intention with your prosperity buddy and write it in your prosperity journal.

2. Record your thoughts about money and their underlying meaning

Once you become accustomed to listening to your thoughts about money, the next step in changing your internal dialogue so a new financial identity can emerge is to uncover their true meaning. To do this, during the day as you begin to notice thoughts that relate to your finances, record them in your prosperity journal then later determine their significance in relation to yourself and others, as in figure 5-2.

3. Select replacement thoughts

Once you understand what you are really saying through your attitudes toward money, you can make a conscious decision to substitute more positive thoughts. List your current thoughts about money, then select a replacement for each unproductive one (see figure 5-3). Keeping in mind the goals you set in Exercise 4, choose thoughts that will support their unfolding.

4. Notice the voices in your head

Determine which characters in your boardinghouse are expressing themselves through your self-talk. The wounded child, rebellious teenager, and critical parent influence most internal dialogue. Using figure 5-4 as an example, correlate thoughts you have with your inner characters and determine how your wise adult might respond to each situation.

5. Usher in a positive character

In addition to acknowledging the guiding role of the wise adult, invite another affirming occupant into your boardinghouse, such as a nurturing goddess who loves you no matter what you think or do, or an ideal father who protects and guides you, or an angel, religious figure, or fictional protogonist or celebrity whose qualities you admire. Most importantly, choose a character who will empower you through praise and encouragement, telling you throughout the day, "You're doing a great job" or "You're terrific!" Ensure that this character lavishes you with praise when you behave productively with your finances by keeping track of your money, avoiding overspending, or saving a small sum.

In addition, evict the critical parent, explaining that the time has come for you to connect consistently with your positive character

Current Thoughts	Meaning
I'm broke.	I'm alone and have no one to turn to.
If I don't pay my bills soon, I'm going to be in real trouble.	I'm a bad person and expect to be punished.
I need to get a credit card with lower interest but don't know how to do this.	I feel trapped by my situation and want someone to help me be more comfortable.
The way I have been spending money is really awful.	I have low self-esteem and need to affirm my self-worth.
I wish I had more money so I could do more things.	I wish there were more people in my life so I could feel more connected.
The way I deal with my money is really stupid.	I'm irresponsible and ashamed of myself.

Figure 5 – 2

Current Thoughts	Replacement Thoughts
I'm broke.	I am capable of accumulating the money I need.
If I don't pay my bills soon, I'm going to be in real trouble.	I will start keeping better track of my money so I don't get into this predicament again.
I need to get a credit card with lower interest but don't know how to do this.	I'm going to find a way to pay off my debt and negotiate a better deal with credit card companies.
The way I have been spending money is really awful.	I'm willing to set boundaries for myself and find out why I need to spend so much.
I wish I had more money so I could do more things.	I'm willing to look at how my focus on money defines who I am and what it actually means.
The way I deal with my money is really stupid.	I have the choice to relate to money differently.

Figure 5 – 3

Thought	Character	Wise Adult
I'm broke and can't buy what I need.	Wounded child	You deserve the best that life has to offer, and we can work together to get you the support you need, apart from money.
I really do a bad job of taking care of my money. No wonder I never have enough.	Critical parent	Let's work together to learn more about money. You are a good person and can have whatever you want.
I'm going to buy the sweater now with my credit card and worry about paying for it later.	Rebellious teenager	If you are willing to wait for the sweater until you can pay cash, you'll feel much better about yourself and develop a healthier financial attitude. What is it you really need right now that you are trying to fix with the sweater?

Figure 5 – 4

to gain confidence. If necessary, imagine helping the critical parent pack and move out, then preparing a departure celebration.

6. Focus on the present

Because a lot of financial fear relates to the future, an unknown prospect, you can develop a more productive mental environment by remaining focused on the present. While worrying about what might happen in the future, ask yourself if you have what you need at the moment, such as enough food for the day, a place to live, and clothes to wear. Such questions will reduce anxiety and prepare the way for more productive thoughts. Next, ask the positive character you have created to help you resolve your concerns about the future. Then decide on a course of action, conduct the necessary research to assess the feasibility of your decision, and move toward resolving your concerns, all of which are healthy ways to prepare for the future while staying focused on the present.

If your mind is occupied with regrets concerning past events, or thoughts about what your parents or others did or did not do, ask yourself how holding on to the past serves to maintain your identity and your current financial position. When it becomes clear that thoughts from the past obstruct your attainment of personal and financial goals, actively decide to let go of them.

7. Use affirmations to release negativity

Affirmations can help replace negative thoughts and profoundly affect many aspects of your life. To transform unproductive thoughts and release fear of changing your identity, choose several affirmations to repeat at various times during the day along with your power word.

Following are examples of useful affirmations:
• I release my need to criticize myself. (Power word)
• I release my fear of changing my thoughts. (Power word)
• I give myself permission to change my thoughts. (Power word)
• I want to change my thoughts. (Power word)
• I can change my thoughts. (Power word)
• I release my need to hold on to the past. (Power word)
• I give myself permission to let go of thoughts of the past. (Power word)
• I am willing to have positive thoughts about myself. (Power word)
• I give myself permission to have positive thoughts about my finances. (Power word)
• I am willing to have positive thoughts about my finances. (Power word)

- I have the right to have positive thoughts about my finances. (Power word)
- I am willing to think of myself as financially secure. (Power word)
- I release my fear of the new person I am becoming. (Power word)
- I have the ability to move my life in a positive direction. (Power word)
- I have whatever I need to live a fulfilling, satisfying life. (Power word)
- I deserve the best that life has to offer. (Power word)

8. Quiet your mind

While in a meditative state, your brain waves slow and it becomes easier to cross from your conscious to your subconscious mind, opening you to deeper levels of intuition and other unconscious resources and abilities. Thus meditating daily can not only quiet your mind, it can train you to focus on the present and help you to connect to your inner wise adult for guidance in creating a peaceful, productive, and prosperous life. If you have never meditated before, begin by doing the following basic exercise for 5 minutes each day, gradually increasing to 20 minutes.

- Choose a clean, quiet place either in your home or out in nature.
- Fold your hands in your lap and close your eyes. Take 10 slow, deep breaths, paying attention to your breath as you inhale and exhale. Then allow your breathing to return to normal as you remain aware of each breath.
- Rather than trying to stop or judge your thoughts, just observe them as if they formed a river and you were standing on its bank watching it flow by.
- As your mind begins to quiet, choose a phrase to repeat to yourself such as "I am in the light and I am filled with the light," "I am peace," or "I am love." If your mind wanders, gently bring it back.

9. Visualize a free-flowing stream of revenue

While meditating, visualize what you hope to achieve as having already happened, thereby stimulating your subconscious mind to help create the circumstances. To improve your financial situation, for example, visualize yourself working at a high-paying job, making wise investment decisions, and generally enjoying a prosperous lifestyle. Using more concrete imagery, you might want to see yourself sailing on a sea of money or in a room piled with gold coins. Or you could visualize yourself in consultation with a financial adviser or financially astute friends who are helping you deal with the money.

As you do this, notice any resistance or discomfort you have and use the power word technique to counteract it. For example, you might say to yourself:

- I give myself permission to have my dreams come true. (Power word)
- I have the power to allow my dreams to come true. (Power word)
- I release my resistance to financial security. (Power word)
- I release my fear of financial security. (Power word)
- I enjoy financial freedom. (Power word)
- I give myself permission to create financial freedom. (Power word)
- My coffers are full. (Power word)
- I have the right to be happy and free. (Power word)
- I release wanting and manifest satisfaction. (Power word)

10. Perform mental exercises with numbers

Since dealing with money requires facility with numbers, doing numerical exercises builds money muscles and helps eliminate habitual thinking. Start with a simple task like multiplying a chosen number sequentially, such as multiplying 8 to arrive at 16, 24, 32, and so forth. Or beginning with 8, add a selected number, such as 5, repeatedly. As mental calculations become easier, tackle a combination of functions, such as adding 5 to a number, then multiplying by 3, and finally dividing by 2.

Writing out more complex mathematical operations also serves to occupy the mind and increase one's acuity with numbers. Start by making up two columns of numbers, ten rows long, and adding them up without using a calculator. Even though we now have many tools for manipulating numbers, working with them manually can increase your willingness to engage with numbers and thus your ability to concentrate on your financial situation.

11. Focus on reaching your goals

Instead of worrying about the past or the future, take action in your mind. Begin proactively replacing time spent fretting about money with stimulating mental activities that can improve your financial skills or reveal new ways to reach your financial goals. Perhaps join with others in making investment decisions or doing financial research. If you don't know anyone with whom you can have this type of conversation, consider participating in an online financial forum or chat room, where you can ask questions and gain new information.

EXERCISE 6

Adopting Functional Financial Beliefs

Every time you spend money, you're casting a vote for the kind of world you want.

—ANNE LAPPE

To develop a long-term healthy relationship with money, it is necessary to have certain beliefs about both your place in the world and money itself. Positive, functional beliefs, such as "I am a successful person," "I can do a good job of taking care of money," or "Wealthy people are generous and trustworthy," contribute to a prosperity mind-set. On the other hand, negative, limiting beliefs, such as "No matter what I do, I can't make enough money," "Wealthy people are greedy," or "I behave badly with money," can block you from reaching your financial goals.

Although culture and family background, along with individual responses to life experiences, all contribute to making a person's set of beliefs as unique as their fingerprints, many people hold similar beliefs related to money and their financial identity. And as it turns out, these beliefs can contribute to financial outcomes.

To facilitate a shift in TBEs that will improve your relationship with money, it is therefore helpful to contrast common limiting beliefs that impede the building of a secure financial foundation with functional beliefs that aid in achieving financial success.

Prevalent Financial Beliefs

Financial beliefs can either limit progress or provide opportunities for growth and prosperity. Common beliefs affecting finances may be divided into four categories, as shown in figure 6-1.

To help uncover your operative financial beliefs so that you can change them, begin paying attention to your thoughts and emotions regarding wealth. Critical statements you might make about what others do with their money or judgments about the character of people in high income brackets would signify negative beliefs you hold about wealth and its consequences. In terms of your own life, if you habitually think about giving away money and respond anxiously to having surplus funds it could be you assume money is the root of all evil and it's noble to be poor—limiting beliefs that are apt to inhibit your ability to build a strong financial foundation.

Methods for Changing Beliefs

Once limiting beliefs are discovered, they can be replaced with functional beliefs that support long-term goals. A simple method for replacing your limiting beliefs is to question their validity, examine how they support your current identity, and face concerns about how new beliefs might change your life. At the same time, be willing to let go of beliefs that restrict progress toward your goals.

Upon finding that you subscribe to the belief "People like me never get rich," for instance, you might identify criteria for "people like me," then go on to read biographies of individuals

Limiting Beliefs

Money	Wealth and Wealthy People	Consequences of Wealth	Financial Identity
Money doesn't grow on trees. A good job is the only path to financial security. Women should never earn more than their male partners. Whoever has the money has the power. People like me never get rich. To make a lot of money, you have to work really hard. Money is the root of all evil.	Wealthy people are greedy. Rich people are arrogant. Wealthy people are different from ordinary people like me. It isn't spiritual to have a lot of money. It's not safe to have a lot of money. Wealth corrupts. It is noble to be poor.	If I have a lot of money, people will see only my money and not my true self. If I'm rich, people will try to get my money. It isn't right for me to make more money than my parents or siblings. If I make a lot of money, I can lose it. If I'm rich, I won't relate to my friends anymore. If I'm wealthy, I can't be spiritual.	I'm a financial failure. I never get what I need. I never get what I want. I don't deserve to be wealthy. People like me struggle financially I'm not smart enough to make a lot of money. Money slips through my fingers. I'll never be wealthy.

Functional Beliefs

Money provides opportunities for growth. Financial security can be attained in many ways. Money and creativity allow us to help others. Money goes to people who love and take care of it. Money can help us overcome difficult life circumstances.	Wealthy people are generous. Wealthy people enjoy life. Wealth and goodness go together. Having more than enough is the best pattern to master. One person's wealth can help others who are disadvantaged.	With a healthy cash flow, I can still be creative and spiritual. With more than enough money, I can have more choices. With more than enough money, I can more easily fulfill my needs and help others.	I am a financial success. I am comfortable financially. I deserve to be wealthy. I have everything I need to build a strong financial base. I am smart enough to make a lot of money. I trust myself to take care of my money. My dreams come true.

Figure 6-1

who have demonstrated these traits and been successful financially, thus invalidating your basic premise and substantiating the truth of a more positive belief such as "People like me are wealthy." In addition, you can ask yourself how holding on to the limiting belief protects your identity, provides an excuse for remaining in your current financial position, and eliminates any need for dealing with the consequences of change. Upon determining that your current belief impedes your progress, you can choose to adopt a more functional belief.

One method for replacing limiting beliefs is the power word technique. Another involves neutralizing their potency with direct action. For example, neutralizing the power of the limiting belief "Money slips through my fingertips" by saving even a small amount of money each week would lead naturally to adoption of the belief "I can control how I use my money." Similarly, budgeting your money so you might take a vacation you have longed for can neutralize the potential paralysis resulting from the belief "I never get what I want." Regardless of the approach used, continually replacing limiting beliefs with functional ones contributes to measurable financial results.

New Beliefs and the Identity Factor

When beliefs begin to shift, the Identity Factor predictably kicks in, due to the changes they foster externally, particularly in terms of behavior. Confusion about what to expect or how to act can cause indecision, disorientation, and declines in confidence. Foreknowledge of such disruptions, along with outreach to a prosperity buddy or people who hold beliefs you are aspiring to, can provide sustenance as you establish a new financial identity.

The morning of her ten-year anniversary as a bookkeeper in a four-person office that "ran like an automated train," Laura wanted out. Though the job had furnished her with an adequate income allowing her to live modestly in a home of her own, Laura had had her fill of the regimentation and longed to trade her just-enough existence for one that accorded her more of life's pleasures.

She suspected that the forces galvanizing her to her desk over the previous decade were beliefs inculcated in her as a child. Brought up in a somber home with three younger siblings, an ultra-strict father who worked long hours as an engineer, and a mother fanatic about order and cleanliness, Laura had come to believe that excesses of any kind were frivolous, if not sinful, including entertainment, dinner parties, and vacation getaways. For as long as she could remember, family weekends revolved around chores and church activities.

When she started working with me, Laura was eager to replace the belief system she had inherited with one of her own choosing, despite the parental disapproval she was sure to encounter. Gradually, she adopted beliefs more aligned with her goals—among them, convictions that she deserved to have fun and that spending money for pleasure was acceptable and desirable. As these began to take root within her, she resigned from her job and started a part-time bookkeeping business that three years later blossomed into a full-time endeavor. With the increased income it provided, she was able to renovate her home, use it for entertaining business associates along with a widening circle of friends, and regularly attend theater productions and concerts. Rejuvenating visits to a nearby health spa motivated her to continue developing new behavior patterns.

Laura's metamorphosis, however, was not always smooth. While struggling to break free of her indoctrinated beliefs, she sometimes felt as if she were teetering on a precipice, in danger of spiraling into a void. And as she moved into uncharted behavioral territory, she occasionally became physically ill or nearly paralyzed by fears of the unknown. Moreover, her parents and two oldest siblings criticized her relentlessly, causing distress she was able to temper by reaching out to her new friends who did not judge her by her family's standards. Fortunately, she knew side effects would accompany any significant identity change and that the discomforts would be temporary—wisdom that helped her emerge radiantly happy with her leap to a level of prosperity offering her abundant opportunities for self-fulfillment.

Actions

The actions for this exercise include suggestions for recognizing and replacing your financial beliefs. Keep in mind that there can be multiple beliefs in effect at any one time and that as you replace one limiting belief, another may rise to the surface, requiring your attention.

1. Examine your financial beliefs

Using figures 6–1 and 6–2 as guides, in your prosperity journal connect your current financial thoughts to your operative beliefs and write down functional beliefs you would like to develop instead. For enhanced outcomes, during meditation ask your wise adult to reveal limiting beliefs that keep you stuck financially. Examine each thought and decide on beliefs that might be supporting it.

2. Question the validity of your limiting beliefs

Write the following questions in your prosperity journal or on an index card that you can carry with you:

Current Thoughts	Operative Beliefs	Replacement Beliefs
I'm broke.	I'm not worthy. I can't have what I want or need. No one wants to support me. I can't support myself.	I am worthy. I can have whatever I want or need. I have the ability to be self-supporting.
If I don't pay my bills soon, I'm going to be in real trouble.	My behavior is shameful. I deserve to be punished. I don't deserve financial comfort. I can't create financial comfort.	I'm a good person. I deserve the best that life has to offer. I deserve financial comfort. I have the ability to create whatever I want.
The way I have been spending money is really awful.	I'm bad. Spending all my money is bad. I'll never have enough to be free.	I'm a good person. I can save money and still have whatever I want. I have the ability to make as much as I choose.
I wish I had more money so I could do more things.	I don't deserve to have what I want. I can't have what I want. I can't have what other people have. I'm poor.	I deserve to have what I want. I can have whatever I want. I deserve the best that life has to offer. I'm worthy.
The way I deal with money is really stupid.	I'm stupid. I never do anything right. I'm a real loser.	I'm smart. I'm competent. I'm successful.

Figure 6–2

- Is this statement true?
- Which part of me believes it is true?
- How does holding on to this belief help me sustain my identity?
- How will letting go of this belief threaten my identity?
- If I were to let go of this belief, how would my life change?
- Am I willing to experience this change?

Each time you recognize a limiting belief that may be blocking you from moving forward financially, dialogue with yourself using this list of questions. Then decide what actions you might take to adopt a more functional belief. To increase the effectiveness of this action, have your prosperity buddy ask you the questions.

3. Use your power word to adopt functional financial beliefs

To adopt replacement beliefs that help drive financial success, employ the following format. Each statement used in conjunction with your power word should be repeated 5 to 10 times.

1. State your willingness to accept the new belief.
2. Give yourself permission to experience its effects.
3. Release your resistance to its effects.
4. Make a positive statement of being.

Here are some examples:

Belief: I am a financial success.

- I am willing to believe that I am a financial success. (Power word)
- I give myself permission to be financially successful. (Power word)
- I release my resistance to financial success. (Power word)
- I enjoy financial success. (Power word)

Belief: Money is a spiritual force.

- I am willing to believe that money is a spiritual force. (Power word)
- I give myself permission to be spiritual and have significant amounts of money. (Power word)
- I release my resistance to being spiritual and having significant amounts of money. (Power word)

- I am spiritual and use significant amounts of money in a spiritual way. (Power word)

Belief: Wealthy people are generous.
- I am willing to believe that wealthy people are generous. (Power word)
- I give myself permission to be a wealthy, generous person. (Power word)
- I release my resistance to being a wealthy, generous person. (Power word)
- I am a wealthy generous person. (Power word)

Belief: With a healthy cash flow, I can have opportunities for growth and creativity.
- I am willing to believe that if I have a healthy cash flow I have opportunities for growth and creativity. (Power word)
- I give myself permission to have a healthy cash flow and opportunities for growth and creativity. (Power word)
- I release my resistance to having a healthy cash flow and opportunities for growth and creativity. (Power word)
- I have a healthy cash flow and opportunities for growth and creativity. (Power word)

4. Create an audiotape or CD to help reprogram your subconscious mind

Recording and then playing back your new beliefs helps to reinforce them. To do this:

- Choose a few statements from your list of functional beliefs.
- Record each statement, speaking slowly and clearly. Repeat it several times.
- Play the tape or CD while falling asleep at night or when you wake up in the morning—times when your subconscious mind

is most receptive. If you fall asleep while listening, your subconscious mind will still hear the words.

5. Examine how the new beliefs affect your identity

With functional beliefs in place, your life cannot help but move in an advantageous direction. To prevent functional beliefs from threatening your identity when they are first introduced, however, imagine the changes that might transpire and your friends' and family's possible reactions to them. Also consider how these changes will affect your concept of who you are and your place in the world, and how you might deal with any discomfort prompted by unfamiliar behaviors. If the new beliefs still end up threatening your identity, release your resistance to them through the power word technique, using such statements as the following:

- I release my need to hold on to old beliefs. (Power word)
- I give myself permission to adopt new beliefs and move forward. (Power word)
- I am willing to adopt new beliefs and change my identity. (Power word)
- I release my fear of moving forward. (Power word)
- I have the right to believe whatever I want. (Power word)
- I am not being disloyal to my friends or family by adopting new beliefs. (Power word)
- I look forward to meeting people who share my new beliefs. (Power word)

6. Implement the new beliefs that support your goals

For each new belief likely to propel you toward one of your financial or lifestyle goals, decide on three action steps you might take to set it in motion. For example, to activate the belief "I can quadruple my net worth in seven years," you might decide to start a business with growth potential; buy, renovate, and sell a distressed property; or join a successful investment club. While composing your action steps, remain alert to any limiting beliefs about your abilities still lurking in the recesses of your mind. Any old beliefs that come to your attention will need to be released and replaced with more functional ones.

EXERCISE 7

Cultivating Healthy
Money Feelings

*They say it is better to be poor and happy
than rich and miserable, but how about a compromise
like moderately rich and just moody.*

—PRINCESS DIANNA

lthough thoughts, beliefs, and emotions exist simultaneously, analyzing them separately provides three different perspectives from which to examine and improve financial situations. The emotional vantage point, in particular, reveals the force with which a person's internal condition can precipitate both wanted and unwanted financial situations. Through examining emotional states and then altering those that inhibit financial growth, it becomes possible to steadily remove blocks and trigger monetary expansion. The modified emotions further reinforce this shift by transforming negative thoughts and limiting beliefs en route to fostering beneficial financial behaviors.

The prevalent habitual emotions expressed through finances—abandonment, shame, anger, deprivation, and sense of being trapped—

are invariably rooted in the past and support an ineffective financial identity. Uprooting these emotions and instead cultivating healthy money feelings allows an expanded financial identity to finally take hold.

How Emotions Create Financial Situations

In *Molecules of Emotion,* Candace Pert refers to emotions as "cellular signals that are involved in the process of translating information into physical reality, literally transforming mind into matter." This statement illuminates, from a physiological perspective, how emotions affect situations we create in our lives, including those associated with finances. In particular, it helps to explain why people who routinely feel good about themselves and supported by others tend to create financial conditions allowing for the experience of freedom and security, whereas those who chronically judge themselves or feel isolated often do not.

Working with emotions as cellular signals, then, shifts the focus from attempting to generate sums of money that will result in pleasant feelings to attaining an emotional state infused with feelings of satisfaction, self-confidence, trust in oneself and others; a willingness to express emotions; and positive expectations about the future. When traits such as these predominate, healthy financial habits emerge naturally, making it relatively easy to produce a positive cash flow and to build surplus funds.

Repressed emotions, by contrast, can have a very negative effect on financial endeavors. Because emotions by their nature seek expression, when they are blocked their energy builds until it is released in indirect, often destructive ways, such as through unpleasant relationships with people or self-defeating financial habits resulting in loss of money. For example, a person who experiences repeated disappointments and refuses to share his feelings with others could also encounter disappointing investment outcomes. Expressing his feelings and developing new expectations and responses, on the other hand, would probably improve his financial situation since his disappointment would no longer need to be expressed through investments.

Acknowledging the causal connection between emotions and finances can help you stop seeing yourself as a victim of circumstances and take action to change your financial condition. At that point, instead of asking, "Why did this happen to me?" you have the option of asking, "What am I expressing through this financial problem?" Imagine, for example, that you have difficulty paying your bills on time. If you ask, "Why does this happen to me?" you might answer that you are underpaid, unexpected expenses keep popping up, or you can't control your spouse's spending, thereby characterizing yourself as a victim of either circumstances or someone else's behavior. On the other hand, if you accept that not paying bills on time provides an opportunity for emotional expression, you can then track the particular feelings stimulated by your behavior, release them, and replace them with more functional feelings.

For many people, merely understanding the emotions they are expressing leads to a shift in behavior and eventually a better financial situation. Forty-year-old Carla, for example, vowed to clear up her credit card debt but each month was unable to pay more than the minimum amount required. Although she enjoyed her work at a public relations firm, her living expenses kept going up while her raises were few and far between. As a result of her financial pattern, Carla felt deprived, trapped, disappointed in herself, and confused about why she could not do more to improve her life.

Upon questioning her, it became apparent that aspects of her personal history were influencing her financial patterns. Carla's parents had rarely encouraged and often criticized her. Moreover, when she was seven her family moved from Germany to the United States, and it was months before she could speak English adequately, making her feel like an outsider, isolated and laden with self-pity. As we looked at her financial situation, Carla realized that feeling sorry for herself was one of her main emotional patterns and that her financial circumstances allowed her to support this habit. She understood that to move forward financially, she had to be willing to replace self-pity with self-trust, gratitude, and feelings of accomplishment.

Using emotional release techniques and teaching herself new feeling responses, Carla was gradually able to alter her emotional landscape and, as a result, establish more productive financial behaviors. Monitoring her progress eighteen months later, she was amazed at the changes: she had become much more confident, had found a better job, and had entirely eliminated her credit card debts. Instead of feeling sorry for herself, Carla now felt satisfied with her new financial identity and the life she was living.

All Feelings Are Valid

Societal judgments about the value of certain emotions as positive or negative, as well as cultural conditioning regarding the expression of emotions, cause many people to deny or repress their feelings out of shame. Phrases like "You shouldn't feel that way," "Boys don't show emotion," or "It isn't spiritual to be angry" reinforce such behaviors. But although emotions can cause states of comfort and discomfort, feelings are not good or bad; they just are. And they serve a purpose—to foster self-expression, trigger behavior, and generally function as a bridge between us and our environment (see figure 7–1). Anger, for example, can signal the fact that someone has violated our boundaries, while excitement and joy may motivate us to move forward.

Figure 7–1 Emotions bridge the internal and external worlds.

People who accept all emotions as valid and find a healthy avenue for their expression are usually able to prevent or solve their financial problems. First, they correlate their dysfunctional financial behaviors, such as compulsive spending or underearning, with uncomfortable emotions; then they release these emotional states and adopt new ones capable of triggering more satisfying financial behaviors.

When the Wounded Child Is in Charge

Many nonproductive financial behaviors result from emotional patterns established early in life. Even with enlightened parents, a child's emotional landscape can include feelings of abandonment, shame, anger, deprivation, and a sense of being trapped—the feelings most frequently prompting uncomfortable financial situations. For example, shame can develop when a child sees herself as smaller and less capable than her parents and older siblings; feelings of deprivation can arise in response to parental discipline; and anger can flare up when a child's desires are unfulfilled. Childhood experiences in less enlightened homes tend to foster deeper emotional wounds. In both instances, the degree to which such wounds affect a person's adult behavior determines their ability to infuse their lives with prosperity.

This does not mean that an uncomfortable childhood will necessarily interfere with a person's ability to generate significant sums of money. To the contrary, such childhood emotions can be the stimulus for building wealth, driving an individual to acquire sophisticated skills and work hard to become a high earner. Until the uncomfortable emotions are addressed, however, it may be impossible to enjoy the wealth and have it promote feelings of security and fulfillment.

Harvey, for example, came from a poor family headed by an alcoholic father who left when Harvey was five. His mother's critical and emotionally distant personality added to his discomfort. When I first consulted with Harvey, he was working as a commodities broker and had a net worth of about $3 million, which he wanted to increase to $6 million in order to feel comfortable and secure. At the same time, he was haunted by a perceived lack of inner purpose and questioned the ethics of his company, where profits mattered more than people.

As a result of the work we did together, he came to understand that fueling his desire for wealth were feelings of abandonment, shame, and deprivation—emotions that had characterized his early life. With this awareness and his willingness to practice the techniques I suggested, Harvey stopped focusing on money and began examining his true desires and values in life. Subsequently he left the financial industry and opened a bicycle store, which enabled him to share his love for exploring the outdoors while building a venture of his own. Following his established financial pattern of creating more than enough money, after a year Harvey succeeded in moving forward financially without the stress and anxiety he had previously experienced. By counteracting much of the childhood programming that had been affecting his finances, he was able to develop into a financially healthy adult.

Outcomes are less triumphant among people who strongly identify with and protect their wounded inner child. For them, the concept of becoming a responsible adult has little appeal because their inner child yearns for freedom and fears that relinquishing control might result in annihilation. Unaware that discipline can lead to more freedom and an increased cash flow, they resist the discipline necessary for establishing healthy financial habits. Fortunately, the commitment to progress can break any habit, allowing a new character—the wise adult—to take charge.

Getting in Touch with Money Feelings

Although people often have difficulty connecting feelings to finances because they are detached from their own emotions, they still have emotional reactions to financial activities. Understanding the nature of these reactions makes it less threatening to recognize them, especially among individuals who equate emotions with outward expressions such as crying and yelling.

Candace Pert, her husband Michael Ruff, Ph.D., and other scientists have found throughout the body cellular receptors through which we experience emotions. A gut feeling, for example, takes place in the abdomen, while the sense of something not quite right can occur in many parts of the body. A sudden tightness in the neck or shoulders, a stomach cramp, heaviness in the arms and legs, a depressed immune system, or a "broken" heart can all signal emotional activity in the body.

Therefore, when examining emotions expressed through finances, instead of focusing on verbal descriptions of emotional states, such as sad, angry, betrayed, or deprived, it is possible to recognize feelings by observing physiological reactions to financial situations. For example, if while purchasing something you know you can't afford, you might notice a gripping feeling around your heart, or a clenching in your abdomen. Because the body signals emotional reactions through its receptors, identifying feelings does not require linguistic sophistication. Merely stating, "I have a tightness in my chest when I think about that" suffices. Such physiological responses alone can help clarify a person's understanding of money feelings so they might change them.

Developing New Emotional Habits

Along the bridge formed between our internal and external worlds, certain situations often trigger predictable feelings. A conversation with a demanding parent, for example, might consistently arouse feelings of anger or shame, while sitting on the beach could induce inner peace. Likewise, financial behaviors, such as receiving or paying bills, asking for a raise, or even making everyday purchases, frequently activate foreseeable emotional responses, which may or may not be uncomfortable. It is the habitual nature of emotional reactions to finances that causes people with improved circumstances to still experience discomfort while making a purchase, paying taxes, or opening an envelope containing a bill. Because this is so, improving your relationship with money requires developing an awareness of not only the habitual feelings expressed through your financial pattern but also those you experience through everyday financial transactions.

With an understanding of your emotional makeup in relation to money, you can begin replacing the emotional responses that no longer serve you with feelings that promote prosperity. This procedure involves three stages: becoming aware of emotions stimulated by financial situations, expressing the emotions, and generating alternate emotions that promote prosperity.

Because emotions define many aspects of your relationship with money, the actions for this exercise are best done over an extended period of time. Most people discover that as they release one emotion expressed through their financial situation, another eventually surfaces, with the periods between releasing emotions becoming increasingly longer and more productive. Indeed, effectively changing habitual emotional responses to financial situations demands at least as much attention and commitment as altering thoughts. Without such a focus, reversion to old patterns that support a well-established financial identity inevitably occurs because emotions act as an expression of identity.

All the while, understand that changing your emotional tone is likely to significantly transform your relationships with others. For example, when a person who habitually acts in a subservient manner replaces his shame or guilt with self-confidence, instead of being easily controlled and seeking to please others he may suddenly set protective boundaries and make more logistic decisions. Such an altered emotional tone requires psychological adjustments and patience with others who might respond as if he were still subservient.

Actions

Since altering emotional responses to financial situations takes determination and courage, before working with the actions that follow, spend some quiet time examining your willingness to change your emotional states. Then declare your commitment to the process.

1. Correlate emotional reactions with financial situations

Emotions similar to those expressed through your financial pattern (see Exercise 3) are likely to be experienced during your daily financial interactions. To correlate your emotional reactions with these situations, do the following activity a few times a week, using a variety of financial situations that normally make you uncomfortable.

- Quiet your mind until you feel relaxed and centered. Then imagine yourself in an uncomfortable financial situation, such as paying a bill, visualizing the situation clearly in your mind.
- As you do this, observe your breathing to see if it accelerates or becomes more labored. Next, focus your attention on your abdomen and notice any tightening or other discomfort. Then scan your head, chest, arms, legs, abdomen, shoulders, and back for signs of discomfort.
- After noticing an uneasy sensation, deepen your familiarity with it by concentrating on its primary characteristic—Is it sharp, dull, tense, shaky?—and its level of intensity.
- Keeping your attention on the sensation, take a few deep breaths, imagining the site of the sensation expanding with each one, and repeat your power word. Or repeat an affirmation, such as "I am willing to let go of this feeling" or "I have no need for this feeling," followed by your power word. If the intensity begins decreasing, continue the procedure until the sensation disappears.
- If instead the sensation persists, provide a pathway for its expression by keeping your attention on it and making a sound to articulate it, such as a deep moan or groan, a growl, scream, or anything else that comes up. Should you encounter some initial reluctance—a response natural to people used to repressing their emotions—persevere until you express the emotion in sound. Then repeat the sound, increasing the volume if possible, until the sensation dissipates.
- When the feeling has disappeared after either the breathing or sound routine, imagine the same financial situation and notice if the feeling reemerges with the same intensity. If it does, repeat the breathing and sound routines, preceded by the statement "I release my resistance to letting go of this feeling," followed

by your power word. Once the feeling has either dissipated or decreased in intensity, proceed to the next step.

• Maintaining your focus on the original financial situation, generate an uplifting feeling as you repeat a positive affirmation, such as "I have plenty of money to pay my bills and enjoy doing this," followed by your power word 5 to 10 times. If the original activity has negative consequences in the real world, such as paying a bill late, visualize instead a positive consequence, like seeing a large balance in your checking account register or paying the bill early as you generate the comfortable feeling while repeating the positive affirmation.

Once you have become familiar with locating feelings in your body while imagining yourself in uncomfortable financial situations, begin tracking your feelings in real-world situations. For example, during a financial interaction notice the sensations in your body, especially the heart and abdomen areas. If you recognize any discomfort, take several deep breaths, silently repeat your power word a few times, and if you wish, say a positive affirmation.

Practice this technique while in situations such as the following:

• Making a purchase
• Discussing finances with someone
• Paying a bill
• Thinking about your debt
• Applying for a mortgage, loan, or credit card
• Talking to someone you consider a financial superior
• Speaking to customers if you have a business
• Keeping track of your money
• Withdrawing money through an ATM machine
• Shopping
• Writing a check

- Executing a stock trade
- Making a financial decision

2. Give your feelings definition

Upon gaining proficiency in observing your sensations during financial transactions, determine the emotion they are expressing, such as feeling abandoned, deprived, ashamed, angry, trapped, or one of the related emotions listed in figure 3–3, on page 61. After recognizing an emotion, release it using the following sequence:

1. Release your need for the feeling.
2. Release your resistance to letting go of the feeling.
3. Affirm your willingness to release the feeling.
4. Give yourself permission to feel something else.
5. Affirm a positive state of being as you imagine experiencing it.

To release the feeling of shame, for instance, you might say:

- I release my need for shame. (Power word)
- I release my resistance to letting go of my shame. (Power word)
- I am willing to release the shame I feel. (Power word)
- I give myself permission to feel pride. (Power word)
- I am proud of myself and what I do. (Power word)

Alternatively, you can use one or more of the following actions to release emotions that may be repressed. Sharing the feelings you recognize with your prosperity buddy can serve as part of the release process.

3. Soothe your inner child

If your wounded inner child frequently finds expression through financial dysfunction, use this technique to heal the child and assist the wise adult in taking more control. The goal is never to

get rid of the inner child, but rather to develop a healthy relationship with this creative, emotional aspect of yourself that loves to
have a good time.

- Sit in a comfortable chair with your eyes closed. Take a few deep
  breaths to relax.
- Imagine traveling deep into your heart, and as you approach
  it, see yourself as a child between the ages of three and five,
  in a large, empty room. At first, you feel isolated and alone;
  then you realize you have special powers and can fill this room
  with whatever you like, such as comfortable pillows to sit on,
  toys to play with, bright images on the wall, and a pet. Spend
  a few minutes creating a room that pleases you and allows you
  to feel safe.
- As you do this, pay attention to the emotional import of the
  decor or the objects you place in the room. If you find you are
  afraid to imagine what you want, determine why and then say
  your power word as you continue decorating the room.
- Now imagine that you as a wise adult walk into the room and
  sit next to yourself as a child. Put your arms around the child
  lovingly and explain that you have come to help. Ask if there
  is anything the child needs, and agree to do your best to fulfill
  these needs.
- Promise to communicate with the child on a regular basis,
  offering reassurances of your love and your eagerness to be
  together again.

At least a few times a week, communicate with the child,
recording the dialogue in your prosperity journal. To reinforce
your link to childhood, use crayons or colored pencils, print
your entry, or write it with your nondominant hand. Naming
and drawing the child can also increase the effectiveness of this
technique.

4. Relate the five major financial feelings to your situation

Using figure 3-3 and the example below as a guide, in your prosperity journal list the five major financial feelings and relate these, where appropriate, to your financial situation.

Abandonment	I often owe people money. I'm underpaid. I lost a lot of money after my divorce. People take advantage of me financially.
Shame	I keep bouncing checks. I'm ashamed about my debt. I never know where my money goes. I'm embarrassed by my income.
Anger	I hate paying so much in taxes. I refuse to pay back money I owe. I pay my bills late because I'm irritated about spending so much. It makes me mad that people with easier jobs earn more than I do. I'm pissed off at myself for not taking better care of my money.
Deprivation	I buy things compulsively, trying to fill an emptiness inside. I feel like an orphan when I think about how little I earn. I hold on to things I don't need. I'd rather be in debt than deny myself the things I want.
Sense of Being Trapped	I feel so locked in by my debt. My job is my penance. I doubt I can ever get out of this situation.

Figure 7–2

While completing this action, allow yourself to feel each emotion, breathing into it as you use your power word and making a sound expressive of it. Then examine every statement you wrote, release self-defeating emotions, and consider more satisfying replacements. For example, if you find that you are ashamed of certain financial behaviors, you can decide to accept your past behavior, let go of the shame, and feel okay about whatever you do. Ceasing self-condemnation can reinforce a more positive self-image and give you the impetus to alter financial behaviors in the future. Similarly, if you feel trapped by a financial situation like debt or insufficient income, you can release the feeling while taking action to create a more productive situation, such as changing your spending habits or looking for a new income source. Doing this for any of your statements clarifies that you have choices and can make functional decisions that move you forward financially.

5. Take a feelings inventory

Once you recognize emotions that are being expressed through your finances, take a feelings inventory to release them. To begin, in your prosperity journal record the feelings you have identified. Then list non-money-related occasions during which you felt this emotion in the past and any traits that contribute to it in the present. For example, if you are aware that you feel shame about your financial behaviors, your list might look something like this:

• I felt ashamed when I broke the neighbor's window.
• I felt ashamed when I failed my spelling test.
• I felt ashamed when I struck out in our Little League game.
• I felt ashamed when I couldn't get a college scholarship.
• I feel ashamed because I'm short.
• I feel ashamed because I'm not very smart.

As you write each statement, reexperience the emotion, breathe into it, and make sounds that express it. Then write or say aloud a release statement followed by your power word, such as these:

• I release my need for shame. (Power word)
• I release my resistance to releasing shame. (Power word)

- I am willing to let go of shame. (Power word)
- I give myself permission to let go of shame. (Power word)
- I release shame and manifest feeling good about myself. (Power word)

Finally, select a past event from your list that had a strong emotional charge. Close your eyes, take a few deep breaths, and imagine the event having a happy ending and yourself experiencing a different feeling as a result. For example, see yourself hitting a home run at a Little League game and simultaneously generate a feeling of exhilaration. Repeat the visualization technique with other events that caused emotional discomfort, always imagining comfortable emotions associated with the altered outcomes.

6. Recognize feelings that support your old identity

Everyone has valid reasons for how their emotional habits developed, most of which are anchored in the distant past. As a result of knowledge gained, most people would probably react differently in similar situations were it not for their investment in maintaining habitual responses that support their familiar identity. Therefore, understanding that new emotional responses can be a threat to your identity and noticing when you resist altering old feeling habits, or make excuses for continuing them, can help you nurture a financial identity characterized by a set of new emotions.

7. Practice new feelings

Because emotions contribute to your financial situation, practicing new feelings (see those you set as a goal in Exercise 4) can help to change it. Feeling satisfied, secure, generous, proud, successful, accepted, and appreciated all characterize the more-than-enough financial pattern, and consciously generating them can therefore usher in congruent situations.

To practice an emotion of your choosing, in a meditative state think back to a time when you experienced it. As you remember the emotion, notice the sensations in all parts of your body and declare what you are feeling. For example, to practice feeling successful, recall a time when you felt successful, even if it was only for a brief period. Clearly imagine the situation that triggered the feeling, allowing yourself to be excited and uplifted. Next say to yourself, "I feel successful." Then silently affirm the feeling, saying, "I am successful." To reinforce these affirmations, follow each one with your power word.

When you are adept at doing this in a meditative state, try it in real-world situations. For example, if you often feel embarrassed by your income, the next time you receive your paycheck take a few deep breaths and imagine feeling satisfied, saying to yourself, "I feel satisfied with the amount I am paid." Although many people fear that if they feel satisfied with what they have in the present they will acquire little or nothing more in the future, the opposite is true: since emotions create financial situations, by practicing feeling satisfied you increase your chances for earning enough to satisfy you. If you have trouble generating the feeling of satisfaction, or any other feeling you are practicing, examine your prevalent emotion and take steps to release it. For example, when attempting to feel satisfied, if all you can feel is angry determine what you are angry about, breathe through the feeling to release it, then replace it with the new feeling of satisfaction.

Establishing Responsible Financial Behaviors

*The way to become rich is to put all your eggs
in one basket and then watch that basket.*
—ANDREW CARNEGIE

For participants in a bodybuilding program, certain related behaviors are likely to emerge naturally, such as eating more wholesome foods, wearing better-fitting clothes, or walking with greater confidence. Similarly, establishing more strength-based thoughts, beliefs, and emotions can lead to more responsible financial behaviors, like taking better care of money, avoiding debt, and planning for the future.

Resistance to unfamiliar actions by an identity threatened with change, however, can retard such progress. This means that while a person could, for example, develop more positive self-talk, expansive beliefs, and comfortable emotions, and consequently raise their quality of life, unless responsible financial behaviors are established as well, a healthy relationship with money will likely remain elusive. The hidden bonus is that as such behaviors become increasingly routine they also usher in a new financial identity.

Adapting to New Behaviors

Virtually every book on personal finance cites guidelines for building financial security: spend less than you earn, get out of debt, save a percentage of your earnings, develop a realistic financial plan, manage your money, and learn about your investment options. While following these guidelines can significantly increase the potential for financial success, doing so means learning new skills and implementing unfamiliar behaviors, which requires stepping into a dark tunnel of transition and inevitably experiencing unpredictable consequences and the disorientation that comes from the moving stupids. With that, many people get discouraged and stay stuck in their financial situation, especially individuals who try to alter too many behaviors in a short time and expect rapid results. Although the morphing process can appear slow to people seeking instant relief from financial troubles, over time even small behavioral adjustments can stimulate dramatic changes. Therefore, as you work through this exercise keep in mind that, like other *Build Your Money Muscles* exercises, it is meant to be part of a long-term program, not a short-term fix.

To minimize resistance to establishing responsible financial behaviors, the actions in this exercise present the most elementary activities needed for developing a profitable relationship with money. Introducing them into your daily routine incrementally over an extended period of time, such as six to twelve months, improves your odds of successfully adapting to new behaviors and unfamiliar results. Additionally, sharing the experience with a prosperity buddy can help significantly to implement the actions because of the support and accountability such a relationship offers.

Further, the actions in this exercise provide practical approaches to achieving the financial goals you set in Exercise 4, Action 1, regarding income, savings, and debt reduction. Now you can realize your goals by:

• Keeping consistent financial records
• Creating a realistic spending plan
• Dealing with your debt
• Developing a savings habit
• Planning for increased cash flow

These activities can substantially alter your relationship with money and lead you to a comfortable financial position as long as you maintain awareness of the potential for resistance and the need to persevere.

Counteracting Resistance

Just as developing stronger physical muscles requires lifting weights or doing other exercises in a disciplined manner over an extended period, building money muscles means following certain financial procedures until they become habitual. Trying to become prosperous without keeping track of your money or spending less than you earn is like trying to lose weight without eating fewer calories or exercising more—it doesn't work.

Unfortunately, many people resist the focus on new skills and discipline required for financial progress, for a number of reasons. One reason is the urge for instant gratification, which propels individuals to purchase things to indulge their momentary fancies, even without sufficient funds, rather than exercise the discipline necessary for sound financial practices. Because managing money can seem dull when compared to enjoying the latest electronic toy or an exotic night on the town, saving for the future or reducing credit card debt frequently plays second fiddle to a fun purchase, despite its tendency to add to financial instability. Ultimately, while it may be enticing to wish for an easier path, the only sure way to tame out-of-control spending and debting or to guarantee a secure financial future is to establish a prudent plan and implement practical money management techniques, which call for discipline, determination, and a strong desire to be more prosperous.

Another reason for resisting the summons to be more responsible financially is fear of losing one's identity along with accustomed positions in one's peer group or family of origin. For people who have had a long-term dysfunctional relationship with money, establishing new financial behaviors means developing unfamiliar personality traits, which can be disorienting and require major adjustments in lifestyle.

Rebecca, for one, yearned for professional recognition and was thrilled when a Los Angeles gallery agreed to display her art. For years, Rebecca had worked at part-time jobs to earn the money she needed for basic living expenses and for art supplies. Rather than attending to her finances, she spent whatever she had available at the moment, occasionally bouncing checks upon losing track of her bank account balance.

When Rebecca's art started selling, each time the gallery paid her she felt a rush of excitement and usually bought something for her apartment or art studio. She had little incentive to change her financial behavior until, after a few months, she realized that the increased flow of money, as wonderful as it seemed, was making her feel obligated to do something else with her surplus. This prompted her to keep better track of her money and open a savings account, where she immediately began putting 10 percent of the proceeds from her art sales. Feeling empowered by her new financial status, she started thinking about purchasing a house and researched mortgages for first-time home buyers.

But after eight months of healthy sales, demand for her art diminished, and Rebecca could see that if something didn't change she would wind up in the same financial position as before her art started selling. As she assessed her circumstances, she became aware that aspects of her life were dragging her back to her old identity.

For one thing, she no longer had the discipline to do financial record-keeping, thereby reverting to her old habit of financial vagueness. For another, she was experiencing difficulties with friends who were unsupportive of her new identity. Then, too, her financial independence had strained her relations with her parents. During most of her adult life, conversations with them had centered on her financial struggles, and missing that kind of attention she became disoriented.

At the same time, Rebecca was confused about how to act toward artists with whom she had previously bonded around the difficulty of gaining financial support in the art world. Although they professed admiration for her growing recognition and sales, she sensed some jealousy and a feeling of separation.

Finally, because she was unprepared for success she had trouble coping with her new status in the art community. Unaccustomed to attention of this kind, she was unsure about how to respond when people complimented her on her art.

Fortunately, as Rebecca started reverting to her old financial identity, she saw what was happening. Determined not to lose what she had gained, she reasserted her financial discipline and was soon back on track with her record keeping. As sales of her art began picking up again, she decided not to succumb to what she now knew as temporary discomforts associated with her new life position but rather maintain the behaviors that could sustain her success. Further, she understood that while she frequently wanted to buy frivolous things to make herself happier, in order to purchase a house she would have to make spending choices. Upon realizing that financial discipline, a concept unfamiliar to her old identity, had its rewards, she began reining in her daily spending to achieve a more important financial goal in the future.

Preparing for Surplus

Most people who hope to improve their financial situation dream of having surplus funds, but relatively few understand the potential effects of generating unfamiliar amounts of money. Although increased funds can indeed contribute to enhanced living conditions, financial positions often remain the same or become less secure because deep-seated emotions, such as shame or deprivation, endure.

Like everything else about money, dealing with a surplus of funds reflects underlying emotional habits. Some people formulate apparently rational reasons for spending the increased income, such as paying off debts, making needed home or automobile repairs, upgrading their living arrangements, buying a new car, or purchasing "needed" products—behavior that maintains a habitual position by leaving no cushion to cover unexpected expenses. Other individuals react to increased cash flow by stashing most of it in a savings or retirement account, thereby establishing emergency funds but too often worrying about losing what they have gained, their anxiety mounting in proportion to the increase in surplus funds.

Midway along the spectrum are people who spend some of the surplus income and use the rest to pay off debt or deposit into a savings account. But even this behavior can cause uncomfortable reactions ranging from paralyzing concern about what to do with the surplus money to frantic activity in search of high-interest investments. Barbara, for example, had little confidence in financial institutions and regularly put a portion of her income in her underwear drawer, which also made her feel uncomfortable. When her cache totaled $7,500, she decided to help her daughter pay off debts, relieved by the prospect of no longer having to decide what to do with her surplus.

Despite the fact that having a surplus of money often contributes to the perpetuation of an earlier financial pattern, planning for increased income before it arrives can help you deal more effectively with potential emotional reactions and face hidden fears that might otherwise trigger a reversion to your previous financial position. Planning for what to do with surplus funds also excites positive thoughts about the future and confidence about financial independence, enabling your subconscious mind to help generate the surplus money.

Planning for surplus means looking at practical options and making multiple decisions about how to manage more money. And before investments or luxuries can be considered, simple conclusions need to be drawn about where to put growing savings and how to allocate incoming funds, all of which can cause feelings of disorientation. Activating new behaviors while planning for surplus money, however, can help avert many of the unexpected discomforts that accompany an enhanced financial positioning, including feeling disconnected from friends or overwhelmed by a sudden inflow of funds.

Actions

The actions for this exercise are designed to help you counteract forces that often impede the development of responsible financial behaviors. Introduce them gradually, always mindful of the potential for emotional discomfort or resistance.

1. Choose new financial behaviors

Identify 5 to 10 habitual behaviors that keep you in your current financial position and select a replacement behavior for each one. For example, if you let bills pile up, decide on a system for paying your bills while simultaneously noticing your emotional responses and determining their significance for future financial success. If you habitually spend more than you earn, develop a sound cash-flow plan and use cash or checks instead of credit. Or if you lend money to others that you could instead be saving, stop making the loans.

To maximize your chances for success, work on changing only one behavior at a time, realizing that since new habits take a while to develop, a changed behavior might temporarily revert to its dysfunctional counterpart. If this happens, accept the reversion without judgment and fully aware that your behavior modification can resume whenever you wish. For further motivation, share your chosen behaviors with your prosperity buddy. Any time resistance sets in, replace the TBEs that might be stirring it up and release your fear of moving forward.

2. Record your progress

Once you begin to implement a new financial behavior, record your progress daily in your prosperity journal to keep yourself on track and reinforce self-confidence. A simple entry such as "Kept track of my spending" or "Did not use my credit card" will suffice, reminding you of your determination to alter habits. Also consider decorating your entry with gold stars or other stickers likely to keep your inner child motivated. After completing the entry, acknowledge your progress verbally, telling yourself, for instance, "You're doing a great job."

For additional support, share your daily entry with your prosperity buddy for a few weeks via e-mail or phone. As a further incentive, decide on a reward to give yourself after implementing a new behavior consistently over a specified period of time, such as writing down your spending every day for two weeks or saving a dollar a day for a month.

3. Calculate your monthly cash flow

An accounting of your monthly cash flow helps you see at a glance your spending and earning patterns. To begin, categorize your expenditures (see figure 8–1) for one month and add up the total in each category, then enter your income for the month from various sources and total it as well. Finally, deduct your monthly expenses from your monthly income. The final figure will indicate if you have a positive or negative cash flow and how much of a surplus or deficit you generated. Using this cash flow report as a guide, you can then adjust your spending to achieve the goals you have set. If you regularly keep track of your money with a financial computer program, at the end of each month generate a cash flow report.

Although this action may seem simple and straightforward, just thinking about comparing income and expenses can set off an intense emotional reaction. If you experience fear or resistance while tallying your monthly cash flow, breathe through whatever reactions arise. As encouragement to complete your cash flow report, discuss it or actually complete it with your prosperity buddy.

4. Adjust your monthly cash flow

To convert a negative cash flow to a positive one, or to increase your surplus, adjust your monthly cash flow—first on paper then

Monthly Cash Flow Report	
Expenses	
Rent/Mortgage	$
Utilities	$
Phone	$
Cable	$
Automobile	$
Insurance	$
Food	$
Medical	$
Clothing	$
Entertainment	$
Travel	$
Taxes	$
Debt repayment	$
Charity	$
Savings	$
Miscellaneous	$
Expense Total	$
Income	
Salary	$
Other income	$
Income Total	$
Income Minus Expenses	$

Figure 8–1

in practice. Using your cash flow report from Action 3, make the desired adjustments by doing the following:

• Determine if any expenses are out of line. For example, are phone or clothing expenses too high, or are you spending too much on entertainment or eating out? If so, find ways to cut back, such as signing up for a less expensive phone plan or making fewer long-distance calls, buying fewer clothes, going to the movies less frequently, or eating at home more often.

- At the same time, consider new ways to generate income, such as holding a garage sale, taking on part-time work, or even changing jobs. If you own your own business, think about changing your marketing strategy, raising your prices, or lowering expenses.

- Calculate how much money you can afford to allocate to debt repayment without leaving yourself strapped. Keep in mind that if you make only minimum payments on credit cards, clearing your debt could take many years. If your debt level is extreme, consider having a credit counselor help you work out a payment plan.

- Estimate how much money you would like to contribute to charitable causes.

- To ensure the gradual accumulation of surplus funds, figure out how much money you can set aside for savings, even if it is only a dollar a week at the outset. Also decide where you will open a savings account once you have fifty dollars and make note of this in your prosperity journal.

- Taking into account all previous considerations, enter the figures you aspire to in an adjusted monthly cash flow report (see figure 8–2). Rectify the totals, where necessary, to arrive at a positive cash flow or your desired surplus. Better yet, enter the chart in a spreadsheet program that allows you see the recalculated final figure each time you adjust a number. Think of your adjusted monthly cash flow report as a plan to activate when you are ready to move to a new level of financial responsibility.

- Choose a date for implementing your adjusted cash flow plan, and as it approaches, examine your feelings about the upcoming changes. If feelings of discomfort or disorientation arise, release them in advance through the techniques described in Exercise 7.

Adjusted Monthly Cash Flow Report	
Expenses	
Rent/Mortgage	$
Utilities	$
Phone	$
Cable	$
Automobile	$
Insurance	$
Food	$
Medical	$
Clothing	$
Entertainment	$
Travel	$
Taxes	$
Debt repayment	$
Charity	$
Savings	$
Miscellaneous	$
Expense Total	$
Income	
Salary	$
Other income	$
Income Total	$
Income Minus Expenses	$

Figure 8–2

5. Initiate goal-directed practices

With an eye toward reaching your financial goals, as outlined in Exercise 4, write a list of simple practices you would like to initiate, at a rate of perhaps one a week, such as eating at home, enjoying a "spending free" day, learning a financial computer program, updating your résumé, or contributing to a charity. If you are in business, list basic practices that can help you achieve your fiscal objectives, such as outlining and implementing new marketing strategies, attending a networking event, or working with a financial coach or bookkeeper. At the end of each week, check off the practice you have introduced and reinforce your sense of progress by envisioning your heart filled with joy or by using a positive phrase to acknowledge yourself while imagining people congratulating you for your achievement.

Also draw up a list of tasks that need to be done regularly and review it at least once a week. Consider including such items as the following:

• Enter all checks and credit card charges into account registers.
• Pay bills as they arrive.
• Balance checkbook upon receipt of statement.
• Save $20 per week.
• Create a cash flow report and review it at the end of the month.

If you use a computer program, utilize the Reminders feature to tell you when to do each of the activities listed above.

6. Deal with your debt

If debting characterizes one of your dysfunctional financial behaviors, giving up the use of credit is one of the most positive things you can do. Eliminating a debting habit requires a strong commitment to becoming solvent and ongoing adjustment in spending routines, coupled with a shift in mind-set. For example, if you view financial responsibility as restrictive, to alter your mind-set you might begin seeing it as an opportunity to accomplish your long-term goals, then reward yourself for progress.

If your debt is significant, consider letting a credit counselor help you restructure it, perhaps at a reduced interest rate, and develop a viable repayment plan by making reasonable arrangements with creditors. Since it is best to entrust your finances on this level to a trustworthy and knowledgeable individual, shop for a credit counselor carefully (see pages 169 and 170 for suggestions).

7. Save some money on a regular basis

A reliable way to start accumulating surplus funds is by regularly putting money into a savings account. To begin, save small amounts daily or weekly. Even a few dollars can generate self-respect and a sense of accomplishment. At the outset, decide what you will do with the money in the future, perhaps allocating some for a specific purpose, such as a vacation, and some for long-term investments.

8. Plan for surplus

As you begin to accumulate extra money, do everything possible to avoid the temptation to spend it, especially if you are unaccustomed to having surplus funds. One fail-safe procedure is to withdraw the excess money from your checking account and deposit it temporarily in a savings account or certificate of deposit (CD), making an agreement with yourself to leave it untouched for a prescribed period of time, such as 6 months, or until it totals a certain amount such as $20,000 or $50,000, at which point it is best to follow an investment strategy. Leaving surplus funds in an interest-bearing account until you feel comfortable investing it will eliminate pressure you might otherwise feel about embarking on a course of action before gathering sufficient information.

If you already have a surplus account and expect to be generating more income but are not sure how to allocate it, interview several financial advisers then select one to guide you effectively in this decision. Also research possible investment strategies, perhaps at your local library or on the Internet. In addition, begin thinking creatively about your financial options. For example, imagine receiving a check large enough to pay off your debts and leave you with an extra $20,000, then decide how you would allocate the surplus among savings, investments, and purchases. Next, picture various other surplus scenarios—such as receiving an annual payment of $50,000, a monthly payment of $1,500, or a lump sum of $200,000—devising strategies for allocating the funds, based on the research you have conducted. Record the plans in your prosperity journal, paying attention to any new behaviors likely to emerge as you actualize these options.

9. Use your power word to shift your TBEs

Staying attuned to the thoughts, beliefs, and emotions produced with each money-related habit you adjust increases the chances of establishing more responsible financial behaviors. Most people feel uplifted and energized as they change their financial habits, although each alteration usually requires a short adjustment period. If during this interval of time you begin resisting a desired change, activate a shift in your TBEs by expressing positive affirmations such as these:

- I release my resistance to moving forward financially. (Power word)
- I release my resistance to assessing my monthly cash flow. (Power word)
- I'm willing to examine my feelings in relation to taking care of my money. (Power word)
- I have the ability to generate surplus funds and take good care of them. (Power word)
- I can find the people I need to help me take care of my money. (Power word)
- I release my fear of getting out of debt and generating surplus funds. (Power word)

- I have the ability to get out of debt and accumulate surplus funds. (Power word)
- I give myself permission to earn more income and accumulate surplus funds. (Power word)

Improving Your Relationships with Yourself and Others

Wealth, like happiness,
is never attained when sought after
directly. It comes as a by-product
of providing a useful service.
—HENRY FORD

Because your current financial situation reflects your relationships with yourself and others, improving these relationships by treating yourself in a more loving manner and widening your circle of friends and aquaintances is an obvious means for increasing your potential for financial success. Productive thoughts, belief in a positive future, authentic emotional expression, and responsible financial behaviors can all enhance your relationship with yourself while attracting others who reflect your evolving TBEs. And just as altering your thoughts simultaneously shifts your beliefs and emotions, adjusting your relationships transforms your mind-set and comes to expression in your finances.

It's All about Support

Awareness of the interconnection between personal support and financial support assists enormously in the mission to achieve prosperity. In times of busyness or confusion, it can keep you on course by reminding you that since financial situations so often mirror personal relationships, supporting yourself and others on every level imaginable manifests naturally in money flow. Owners of small businesses see such reciprocity in action when customers who have been treated well repeatedly patronize their stores or services. By contrast, people who feel disconnected from others and without a support system are often plagued with money worries. In fact, many habitually underpaid individuals believe they were never supported by peers or family members. Because of the profound influence of support, nurturing relationships with yourself and others is fundamental to changing your financial position.

In general, a focus centered on three main areas of support—physical, emotional, and spiritual—leads to significant financial improvements. Physical support entails giving the body what it requires to function effectively and remain healthy. This means eating moderate amounts of fresh, whole foods; taking supplements when necessary; drinking plenty of pure water; exercising regularly; getting enough sleep; and treating the body in a loving way. Physical support also extends to external factors, such as the comfort of clothing and shoes, the condition of housing, and indoor and outdoor air quality. Following a regimen supportive of the body's well-being provides the energy needed to optimize physical and mental performance and to reduce or eliminate medical costs, ultimately serving the cause of financial progress.

Emotional support refers to being authentic about feelings, overcoming fear of self-expression, setting boundaries for self-protection, and learning to not take things personally. It also calls for the development of emotions congruent with a prosperous lifestyle, such as feelings of security, satisfaction, confidence, and self-respect, and a willingness to let go of neediness, shame, and other feelings that undermine self-worth and financial success. In addition, emotional support includes accepting, appreciating, and respecting yourself—in effect, becoming your biggest fan.

Spiritual support means deepening one's connection to the inner self and developing knowledge of the self as part of an inter-connected whole. Such understanding leads to a perception of money as an energy force that has the potential to flow freely from person to person, awakening the experience of abundance for all who are willing to see beyond self-imposed limitations. Thus, spiritual support perpetually sparks the realization that love, sharing, forgiveness, and compassion foster financial flow while fear, greed, judgment, and hoarding block it.

Providing support in all three areas paves a direct route to financial support. Creating the various conditions, however, may require altering multiple habitual behaviors, an endeavor that can take months, or even years, to accomplish. Fortunately, progress is apparent every step of the way since a person's financial identity morphs into something new with each incremental change.

Treat Yourself Like Someone You Love

Because TBEs manifest circumstances, people who focus on taking care of themselves, including their fiscal well-being, are likely to attract situations in which they are well cared for. From this perspective, the end result of loving yourself can be generating more income. Treating yourself like someone you love in order to make significant progress toward a more secure financial position includes engaging in positive self-talk, letting go of self-judgment, forgiving yourself for unwanted behaviors in the past and present, giving your body, mind, and spirit high-quality care, and seeing yourself through loving, compassionate eyes. Most people who do this automatically treat others differently too, and as a result, elicit more supportive responses from the world around them.

Jerry, for example, began to treat himself in a more loving manner, even though the idea initially seemed schmaltzy to him and incongruous with his competitive work as a real estate agent. First, he focused on replacing the critical voice in his head with one that sounded like his high-school football coach, who had often praised him, all the while encouraging him to improve himself. Then he paid more attention to his diet; joined a gym, where he worked out three times a week; and implemented a home practice of meditating for twenty minutes every morning before starting his workday. Soon he noticed that he felt better at the office and his attitude toward clients seemed more congenial and accepting. Although he made only a few changes in his marketing strategy, referrals began flooding in, more than ever before, and closing deals became less stressful. After about six months, Jerry realized he was not only feeling a lot better and making more money but also having much more fun—presenting a compelling case for how treating oneself lovingly can further well-being *and* prosperity.

Trust Yourself

Effectively dealing with increasingly large sums of money requires developing trust in yourself and your decisions. Despite people's fantasies about sudden inflows of cash, those whose financial pattern is to have just enough or less than enough money often do not trust their ability to make wise decisions about allocating the funds. If this is true of you, one way to develop more trust is by increasing your knowledge of money management. As you build confidence in your ability to protect yourself financially, you are likely to simultaneously stop worrying about others taking advantage of you or about making serious mistakes that can lead to significant financial loss.

Increased trust can also be developed by expressing your authentic self and by setting protective boundaries. Although taking such steps is sometimes frightening, especially for people accustomed to limited self-expression and boundaries made to please others, the payoff can be immense in terms of self-confidence. Two simple statements can help you discover your authentic self and ask for what you honestly need: "'No' is a complete sentence" and "If one of us must be uncomfortable, it doesn't have to be me." The first statement gives you permission to say no without explanation and thus actively determine the events of your life. The second statement promotes decision making that is in your best interest rather than someone else's. Many people find that when they begin looking out for themselves they feel better about who they are and notice improved self-support in many areas of their lives. With that, there develops a new sense not only of trust but of deserving, along with more responsible financial behaviors and, invariably, expanded income.

As for setting protective boundaries to build trust, ideally these are established with respect to both oneself and others. Personal boundaries might include placing limits on spending, avoiding sugar-laden foods, disallowing negative self-talk, or making a commitment to tithe a specific percentage of your income. Boundaries regarding others could include refusing to tolerate language or behavior that you consider inappropriate, asking telemarketers to stop calling you, or saying no to persistent salespeople.

Finally, self-trust in terms of finances can be developed by consciously making small changes in the way you handle your money. Keeping track of cash flow, regularly balancing your checkbook, cutting down on frivolous spending, saving a sum every month, and other responsible financial behaviors are likely over time to convince you that you can indeed be trusted with money.

Connect to Others

Because money is attached to people, connecting to others becomes an essential activity for improving financial situations. Consequently, beyond treating oneself lovingly, developing self-trust, and setting personal boundaries, the fostering of financial security in an unsafe world calls for establishing a network of trustworthy individuals who instill a sense of safety and security. After assembling such a network, people usually feel supported and begin to trust that life will provide the resources required to fulfill their needs. From this vantage point, it would make sense for individuals sitting at home and wondering how to generate more money to begin creating a network of supportive colleagues and for people who already have a wide circle of acquaintances or business associates to deepen those relationships.

While focusing on networking, remember that money does not necessarily come from the people with whom you make contact. Rather, it is through sharing yourself with them that you broaden your sphere of influence and increase the potential of helpful financial interactions. At the same time, as a result of making meaningful connections you will probably feel more loved and supported, both of which routinely stimulate increased cash flow.

Many opportunities exist for enhancing interactions with others, including participation in organizations affiliated with religious institutions, business networking groups, sports teams, discussion groups, Twelve-Step programs, or cultural events. Although less intimate than face-to-face contact, the Internet too provides forums for connecting with other individuals, especially in chat rooms.

For many people, this exercise represents a major shift in personal focus and therefore demands strong dedication. If you are unaccustomed to concentrating on loving yourself and reaching out to others, expect waves of disorientation. But also recognize that as they wash out to sea and you persevere in your mission, your efforts, like those of an oyster making a pearl from the irritation of a grain of sand, are sure to burnish a new identity—in this case, one poised for increased financial rewards.

Actions

The main goal of this exercise is to develop more loving, supportive relationships with yourself and others as a pathway to improving your relationship with money. While working with the actions that follow, however, do not be surprised if you notice an abundance of other joys.

1. Commit to a relationship with yourself

A relationship with yourself is essential for success. After establishing one, the next step is to actively nurture it by giving yourself the love, acceptance, and appreciation that also lead to increased cash flow.

Using the following questions as a guide, think about what it might mean to commit to making your relationship with yourself a daily priority.

• How would I behave if I were committed to my relationship with myself?

- What might I do to show that I care for myself?
- How much time and effort would I be willing to invest in the relationship?
- How will an improved relationship with myself affect my position in my peer group and family of origin?
- How might a committed relationship with myself affect my self-image?
- What might keep me from committing to my relationship with myself? How would I deal with this issue?

When you are ready to prioritize your relationship with yourself, celebrate the commitment, perhaps with a festive dinner out on the town with a friend. Also share the commitment with your prosperity buddy and document it in capital letters in your prosperity journal.

2. Treat yourself in a loving way

Many people fantasize about how they would like to be treated by a loving partner without realizing that they can give themselves what they hope to receive. In addition to the good feelings it generates, treating yourself as special allows for satisfying interdependent rather than unfulfilling codependent love relationships.

To begin treating yourself more lovingly, notice how you currently behave toward yourself in various situations, then replace demeaning words and actions with caring ones. For example, if you rarely compliment yourself when finishing a task, start expressing appreciation for your efforts.

At the same time, begin affirming your love and support for yourself every day. While standing in front of a mirror, you might look into your eyes and say, for instance, "[Your name], I unconditionally love, accept, and support you just the way you are." Whatever your affirmation is, pay attention to the emotions it evokes within you and their possible contribution to your self-esteem and financial mobility.

Additionally, make a list of things you wish someone would do for you and determine which items you can perform on your own. Your list might look something like this:

- Buy me flowers.
- Take me out to dinner.
- Appreciate me.
- Tell me I'm wonderful.
- Love my body.
- Tell me I look good.

3. Reach out to others

Your current level of comfort with other people will probably determine the pace at which you broaden your circle of contacts without feeling threatened. If insecurity about social skills causes you to isolate yourself, to begin bonding more closely with others you may have to face an underlying fear of strangers and an expectation of disapproval. A good way to work through it is to visit unfamiliar places with your prosperity buddy or with another friend hoping to broaden their network of support.

Effective means for reaching out to others include these:

- Attending seminars, discussion groups, Twelve-Step meetings, or professional conferences offering safe environments for sharing ideas and concerns.
- Volunteering at hospitals or nonprofit organizations, where you can function as part of a group in a structured situation.
- Joining a service organization, such as Rotary, Kiwanis, or Lions Club, that provides opportunities for community involvement.
- Becoming a mentor to a young student.

4. Visualize the ideal situation

While meditating, visualize yourself surrounded by caring people and imagine your heart swelling with love. The particular scenario might be one of these or any other of your choosing:

- People praising you for your accomplishments
- Receiving an award for performing a community service
- Participating in a fun project with others
- Attending a meeting with like-minded people and feeling comfortable
- Singing in a choir
- Having a meaningful conversation with someone you admire

5. Do something every day to improve your relationships

Photocopy figure 9–1, adding other activities that appeal to you. Then keep it in a prominent place as a reminder to do something each day to deepen you connections with yourself and others.

6. Use your power word to encourage change

Since changing your relationships with yourself and others involves deep-seated transformations, rigorously exercise the "muscles" that help you overcome resistance to altering your daily routine. Because overcoming resistance requires determination and encouragement, use affirmations such as the following:

- I give myself permission to be my first priority. (Power word)
- I am willing to treat myself in a loving way. (Power word)
- I release my need for isolation. (Power word)
- I release my fear of connecting with unfamiliar people. (Power word)
- I give myself permission to connect with others fearlessly. (Power word)
- I can give freely to others and still feel safe. (Power word)

Improving Relationships with Self and Others	
Spend time with yourself every day.	Drink plenty of pure water.
Make yourself your first priority.	Breathe and center yourself.
Treat yourself like someone you love.	Eat healthy, colorful foods.
Forgive yourself and others.	Get a good night's sleep.
Be honest and accepting about who you are.	Be willing to let go.
Take care of your money.	Clear your clutter.
Say no when you want to.	Pet a dog or cat.
Have fun and laugh.	Give time and money to others.
Save energy and money for yourself.	Be kind to others.
Praise yourself.	Be patient with others.
Be patient with yourself.	See others as wounded children who need your love.
Learn something new about finances.	Be nonjudgmental.
Appreciate yourself.	Support others in being who they are.
Express yourself.	Be available to others.
Fire your critical parent.	Smile at someone you don't know.
Play with and love your inner child.	Compliment a friend.
Go for a brisk walk.	Offer a stranger a helping hand.

Figure 9–1

- I am willing to connect with others. (Power word)
- I release my need to judge myself and others. (Power word)
- I am willing to forgive myself. (Power word)
- I am willing to forgive anyone who I believe has hurt me. (Power word)
- I am willing to do something nice for myself that I have never done before. (Power word)

- I am lovable and loved. (Power word)
- I release my resistance to healthy habits. (Power word)
- I release my need for resistance. (Power word)
- I am willing to move fully into my new financial identity. (Power word)

Despite the effort needed to overcome resistance, surmounting it will result in greatly increased potential for your financial future.

CONCLUSION

Maintaining Your New Financial Identity

This program for financial fitness, like any beginner-friendly routine for optimizing core physical health, requires a lifetime commitment. Short-term, however, only small increments of time are needed—all dedicated to strengthening and securing your emerging financial identity. In the end, it is not so much the *amount* as the *consistency* of attention given to caring for your money and yourself that determines the difference between continued financial success and a return to old, dysfunctional habits.

On a daily basis, ten to thirty minutes allocated to financial management is usually sufficient for fortifying a burgeoning financial identity. For best results, consider attending to these tasks at the same time each day, such as first thing in the morning or at the end of your workday. Begin by entering into your financial computer program checks written, credit card charges accrued, and income earned. Pay bills as well, and schedule the payment of newly arrived bills. If your bank or credit card statement has recently arrived, also reconcile the account, a procedure that takes only a few minutes with financial software, especially if you have been faithfully entering monies spent and earned. Every time you perform one of these tasks, monitor your TBEs and alter any that might be holding you back. If while reviewing your credit card statement you feel ashamed or guilty about the expenses recorded, for example, plan to replace your purchasing-on-credit habit with more responsible behaviors, such as writing checks or paying cash for items.

Weekly, caring for your money calls for the same sort of efficiency. First, remember to generate a cash flow report, then analyze the relationship between your income and expenses and adjust your spending if necessary. In addition, devote an hour or two to reading financial publications; conversing about investments with friends, your prosperity buddy, or a financial adviser; and researching investment opportunities, paper trading, or making actual investments. All the while, continue to notice your thoughts and feelings about money, releasing any negativity or discomfort that arises.

Along with the weekly and daily tasks you undertake to support your shifting financial identity, some surprises may crop up as well. You might find yourself cleaning out closets, for instance, or upgrading furniture, updating your Rolodex, shopping at unfamiliar stores, moving to a new house or apartment, or widening your circle of friends. Try not to be disturbed by these or other unplanned behaviors; rather, see them as indications that you are in fact changing. In becoming, as the twentieth-century spiritual philosopher Jiddu Krishnamurti often suggested, both the observer and the observed, you detach from your old identity and make way for the new one.

Another result of actively maintaining your emerging identity is increased assurance about the financial decisions you make. With continued progress, you are likely to wake up to the realization that the entire spectrum of financial potential is open to you. And indeed, whatever you dream of achieving is yours, whether you wish to amass great wealth or simply to increase your net worth by a modest amount that will allow you to enjoy more of life's gifts. You need only keep on track by continually deepening your relationship with money and with yourself. You deserve the best that life has to offer—so be sure to reach for it.

Resources

RECOMMENDED WEB SITES

General Information
Prosperity Placc—www.ProsperityPlace.com
   Free articles, e-books, audios, and the monthly e-zine Prosperity Tips

Financial Portals
CBS's finance site—www.CBSMarketwatch.com
CEO Express—www.ceoexpress.com
CNN Money—www.cnnmoney.com
MSN Money—www.moneycentral.msn.com
Yahoo's finance site—www.finance.yahoo.com

Insider Tips
About.com's Credit/Debt Management section—
www.credit.about.com
   Instructions for reducing debt, dealing with creditors, and removing items from credit reports
BankRate.com—www.BankRate.com
   Rates for savings accounts, CDs, and mortgages, plus useful articles
Codependents Anonymous—www.coda.org
   A Twelve-Step program for resolving relationship issues
Consumer Credit Counseling Service—www.nfcc.org
   Also known as National Foundation for Credit Counseling, a non-profit organization that assists in finding reputable credit counselors
Debtors Anonymous—www.debtorsanonymous.org
   Help for people with a debting problem

Federal Trade Commission's Credit Web Site—
www.ftc.gov/bcp/conline/edcams/credit/index.html
*Practical articles about credit and debt management, including how
to find a reputable credit counselor*
Financial Power Tools—www.financialpowertools.com/
Calculators to help with financial planning and strategizing
Free Credit Report—www.annualcreditreport.com
Free annual credit reports
iVillage.com's Money section—www.ivillage.com/money
*Information about dealing with debt and investing, as well as links
to support groups*

Free Investment Facts and Figures
Investopedia.com—www.investopedia.com
Good investment dictionary and tutorials for beginners
MorningStar—www.Morningstar.com
Helpful articles, charts, and ratings for mutual funds
Motley Fool—www.fool.com
*An excellent starting point, with articles about investing, credit,
retirement, and other financial topics*
Optionetics—www.Optionetics.com
*Free articles, charts, options pricing, forums, and weekly newsletter
for novices wanting to learn how to trade options*

Subscriptions
Cheapskate Monthly—www.cheapskatemonthly.com
*An inexpensive monthly publication offering excellent information
about basic money management and wise spending*
Investor's Business Daily—www.investors.com
*A daily periodical presenting investors with a wide range of research
tools*
The Wall Street Journal—www.wsj.com
The online edition of this popular financial newspaper

Suggested Reading

Belsky, Gary, and Thomas Gilovich. *Why Smart People Make Big Money Mistakes and How to Correct Them.* New York: Simon & Schuster, 1999.

Bradley, Susan. *Sudden Money: Managing a Financial Windfall* New York: John Wiley & Sons, 2000.

Bradshaw, John. *Healing the Shame That Binds You.* Deerfield Beach, FL: Health Communications, 1988.

Capacchione, Lucia. *Recovery of Your Inner Child.* New York: Simon & Schuster, 1991.

Chatzky, Jean. *You Don't Have to Be Rich.* New York: Penguin Group, 2003.

Chopra, Deepak. *The Seven Spiritual Laws of Success.* Novato, CA: New World Library, 1993.

Covey, Stephen R. *The 7 Habits of Highly Effective People.* New York: Simon & Schuster, 1989.

Eker, Harv T. *Secrets of the Millionaire Mind.* New York: Harper Business, 2005.

Hill, Napoleon. *Think & Grow Rich.* New York: Fawcett Crest, 1960.

Hunt, Mary. *Debt-Proof Living: The Complete Guide to Living Financially Free.* Nashville, TN: Broadman & Holman, 1999.

Jeffers, Susan. *Feel the Fear and Do It Anyhow.* New York: Ballantine, 1988.

Kinder, George. *The Seven Stages of Money Maturity: Understanding the Spirit and Value of Money in Your Life.* New York: Dell, 2000.

Kiosaki, Robert T. *Rich Dad, Poor Dad.* New York: Warner Books, 1999.

Mundis, Jerrold. *Making Peace with Money.* Kansas City, MO: Andrews McMeel Publishing, 1999.

Murphy, Dr. Joseph. *The Power of Your Subconscious Mind.* New York: Bantam Books, 2001.

Nemeth, Maria. *The Energy of Money: A Spiritual Guide to Financial and Personal Fulfillment.* New York: Ballantine, 1998.

Nims, Larry, and Joan Sotkin. *Be Set Free Fast!* Santa Fe, NM: Prosperity Place, 2002.

Orman, Suze. *The Courage to Be Rich: Creating a Life of Material & Spiritual Abundance.* New York: Riverhead Books, 1999.

Pert, Candace. *Molecules of Emotion: The Science Behind Body-Mind Medicine.* New York: Simon & Schuster, 1997.

Ruiz, Don Miguel. *The Four Agreements: A Practical Guide to Personal Freedom.* San Rafael, CA: Amber-Allen Publishing, 1997.

Stanley, Thomas J. *The Millionaire Mind.* Kansas City: Andrews McMeel, 2000.

Twist, Lynne. *The Soul of Money: Transforming Your Relationship with Money.* New York: W. W. Norton, 2003.

About the Author

Joan Sotkin—a sought-after speaker, coach, and seminar leader—maintains a strong online following through tele-seminars and e-books, as well as directing prosperity groups and writing a monthly newsletter for over 100,000 subscribers worldwide. But things weren't always rosy for this entrepreneur. In the late 1980s, after building Joan's Crystals, her mail-order and retail outlet based in Venice, California, into a lucrative enterprise, she went bankrupt. Eight years later, at age fifty-six, having been prompted to relocate to Santa Fe, New Mexico, with a mere two hundred dollars in her pocket, she began to hone her money muscles. Today, she calls upon her decades of financial, physical, and spiritual struggle, along with her hard-earned business acumen, to counsel others in finance so they, too, might achieve lasting prosperity.

The Complete
Build Your Money Muscles Program

Reading *Build Your Money Muscles* is step one in taking charge of your money and creating a successful financial identity. Targeting the most vulnerable areas of concern through this companion program is step two.

The *Build Your Money Muscles* program offers ongoing support through e-books, articles, audio, and teleclasses, all designed to help you reach your financial and lifestyle goals.

Here you will find trade secrets for overcoming fear of success, fear of failure, long-established financial dysfunction, and other blocks to success. With these state-of-the-art techniques, you can move beyond the confines imposed by silenced emotions, while energizing your emerging financial identity.

Also included are detailed instructions for developing new income streams, such as how to choose and grow a full- or part-time business that is right for you.

Find out more about the program and its benefits by logging on to:

www.BuildYourMoneyMuscles.com/1002/

**While there, be sure to download your free copy
of the forms appearing in this book.**

Free Ongoing Support

There's a vast support system at your disposal when you log on to ProsperityPlace.com. Here you'll find a bounty of *free* help through the popular e-mail newsletter *Prosperity Tips*, along with articles, e-books, and audio recordings all designed to empower the growth of an identity destined for financial and personal success.

At ProsperityPlace.com, you can learn mind- and energy-enhancing techniques used by holistic healers around the world. Tapping into your subconscious mind through Be Set Free Fast (BSFF) developed by Larry Nims, Ph.D., and the Emotional Freedom Techniques (EFT) created by Gary Craig, for instance, enables you to quickly clear any number of internal blocks and discomforts. Many proponents of these state-of-the-art techniques consider them more powerful than professional counseling.

Or you can visit ProsperityPlace.com simply to sign up for *Prosperity Tips*. As a subscriber you will receive, at least once a month, an insightful article providing ideas to implement, as well as book reviews, financial strategies, and news about money issues that affect you personally.

Learn more about these free resources by logging on to:

www.ProsperityPlace.com

Order Form

QUANTITY		AMOUNT
_____	*Build Your Money Muscles: Nine Simple Exercises for Improving Your Relationship with Money* (hardcover $24.95, paperback $18.95)	_____
	Sales tax of 7.7% for New Mexico residents	_____
	Shipping & handling (hardcover: $4.50 for first book, $1.50 for each additional book; paperback: $3.50 for first book, $1.00 for each additional book)	_____
	Total amount enclosed	_____

Quantity discounts available

Method of payment

❐ Check or money order enclosed
(made payable to **Prosperity Place, Inc.** in US currency only)

❐ MasterCard   ❐ VISA

Card #_____ Expiration date_____

Signature _____

Please contact your local bookstore or mail your order, together with your name, address, and check, money order, or charge-card information, to:

Prosperity
Place

Prosperity Place, Inc.
PO Box 22993
Santa Fe, NM 87502
Phone toll-free: 888-779-5626